ONE WEEK LOAN

D1494134

Boundary Disputes
A Practical Guide

by
William Hanbury
Barrister, Zenith Chambers, Leeds

EMIS Professional Publishing Ltd

© William Hanbury 2003

Published by
EMIS Professional Publishing Ltd
31–33 Stonehills House
Howardsgate
Welwyn Garden City
AL8 6PU

ISBN 1 85811 301 6

Typeset by Jane Conway
Cover by Jane Conway

Printed by Print Solutions Partnership

Contents

Foreword

Boundary disputes have been described as "a particularly painful form of litigation"[1] and it is the modest aim of this book to make them less so for the practitioner if not for the litigant. They are painful because the law is complex and because "there are few disputes that raise passions more".[2] In my experience only those arising out of car parking are more acrimonious.

Many lawyers are content to assume that their clients will live with a certain amount of vagueness in relation to the precise boundary between their and their neighbour's property. Unfortunately their clients, who assume that the boundary may be determined with absolute precision, often do not share this assumption. So it is my unfortunate task to assist with the task of rendering clear that which is inherently vague.

This book begins with a discussion about the conveyancing documents by which title to the disputed land is obtained and ends where many boundary disputes end: with litigation and the remedies which are likely to flow from that litigation. In between, I analyse the various signposts that exist on the way to identifying the correct boundary position and consider how a boundary may change as a consequence of the operation of the law of limitation, in certain circumstances by the agreement of the parties and by accretion and erosion in the case of a property that adjoins a watercourse.

At least it can be said of boundary disputes that there is usually a right answer and a wrong answer. Unfortunately that answer may lie buried beneath the plethora of evidence, sometimes conflicting, which is characteristic of this type of litigation. I offer some guidance in the type of evidence that might be relevant to resolving a boundary dispute as well as dealing with the vexed question of expert evidence.

For those who wish to spend 22 days litigating over six flower pots and an alleged infringement of 3" by their neighbour over their boundary (the principal cause of the dispute in *Rimmer* v *Pearson*[3])

---

1   *Per* Lord Hoffman in *Alan Wibberley Building Ltd* v *Insley* [1999] 1 WLR 894.
2   *Per* Peter Gibson LJ in *Clarke* v *O'Keefe* (2000) 80 P & CR 126.
3   (2000) 79 P & CR D 21.

I hope this book helps them in their task. For those who wish for sound practical advice on how to avoid a boundary dispute, I hope this book will also help them in theirs.

Table of Cases

Table of Statutes

Introduction

A boundary is an artificial line which divides two contiguous pieces of land. A physical feature such as a wall may mark that line or it may have no marking. Boundaries may be natural or artificial according to whether or not the physical objects marking the boundary are man-made.[1] Boundaries may be horizontal or vertical and may be fixed by the agreement of the parties, by statute or statutory instrument or in the absence of these, by legal presumption.

The complexities of the subject may be better understood if it is remembered that there is no such thing as absolute title. All title is relative and all disputes of this kind depend on one person showing that he has a better title to land than anyone else. The concept of "title" is in reality a bundle of rights which flow from actual possession of the land in question. The extent to which title may be said to be absolute depends on the degree of factual possession of the land. Hence confusion may arise for the layman when absolute title is registered. Such title is liable to interruption by those who can show a better title.

Nevertheless freehold title provides a relatively secure form of ownership. The Government have recognised this and built on the legal and psychological advantages of freehold by introducing a new form of ownership, known as "commonhold".[2] This new commonhold ownership will make provision for owners of flats and other interdependent units, including the common parts of the buildings of which those units form part, to be managed collectively.

Of greater interest to readers will be the Land Registration Act 2002,[3] which contains important changes to the law of adverse possession as well as the law relating to the registration of cautions and protection of interests on the Register generally. That Act, which is not in force as this book goes t press, will also establish the framework for

---

1 *Mackenzie v Banks* (1878) 3 App Cas 1324.
2 Introduced by the Commonhold and Leasehold Reform Act 2002, which received Royal Assent on 1st May 2002 and will come into force on a date to be fixed by statutory instrument.
3 The new Act received Royal Assent on 26th February 2002 and is likely to come into force in October 2003, although at the time of writing a date has not been fixed. By virtue of section 136 the Lord Chancellor may fix different dates for different purposes.

the introduction of electronic conveyancing, which is likely to be of great significance to conveyancing in the future. Although electronic conveyancing may affect the way conveyancing is carried out with potential benefits in terms of speed and cost savings, boundaries (and the rather arcane rules with which they are sometimes determined) are unlikely to change significantly.

As well as changes in the substantive law, which appear to be significant, there continues to be a shift away from court-based methods of dispute resolution towards alternative dispute resolution. The courts now encourage ADR to the extent that a litigant who fails to refer a dispute capable of resolution to, for example, mediation may be penalised in costs.

The perception of most judges appears to be that both sides are equally to blame for boundary disputes when they arise. They are rarely regarded by the judiciary, especially the county court judiciary, as a priority for the use of their judicial time. It is unfortunate that disputes that are frequently regarded by judges to be a matter of knocking heads together are in fact often disputes, which require careful analysis. That analysis is better carried out with at least background knowledge of conveyancing and Land Registry practice. Where possible therefore I set the relevant law against that background.

The trend is to simplify and modernise conveyancing and it is to be hoped that this trend will continue. But although conveyancing is now essentially governed by statute and is dominated by the principles pertaining to registered land it is also necessary to have some understanding of the estates and interests which existed at law and in equity before the 1925 property legislation and for these the reader is referred to the principal works on the subject.[4]

The chapters that follow therefore consider the common law and equity, the cases and statutes, which make up a diverse but practically important subject. They are intended as a practical guide rather than as an authoritative analysis of the law, particularly for the litigation or conveyancing practitioner who wishes to find most of what is required in one place. The law is accurate at the 31st January 2003.

---

4   See Megarry and Wade '*The Law of Real Property*' 6th edition and Gray '*Elements of Land Law*' 3rd edition.

CHAPTER 1

The conveyance or transfer

The conveyance or transfer

1.1
Introduction

The starting point for the establishment of the correct boundary position is the description of the parcels in the conveyance or transfer. Where a dispute arises as to the meaning of the parcels it is frequently necessary for the practitioner to devise a root of title from the earliest conveyance up to the present time. Apart from the fact that this laborious approach is unavoidable, it is also usually revealing because in the past (by which is meant before land registration) conveyances were frequently drafted with greater care than they are now. Secondly, discrepancies between conveyance and plan (which are often repeated from generation to generation) may sometimes be resolved by this process.

Older deeds are often called "indentures" because the old practice was to write out the deed twice on a single sheet of parchment. The parchment was then severed and each party retained one half of the complete sheet of parchment. The two halves could be pieced together to show that the deeds were genuine. It was called an "indenture" because each sheet had an indented edge. The modern practice is to call the deed by which title is passed in the case of unregistered land a "conveyance".

A deed of conveyance contains the following:

- The commencement date;

- The names of the parties and the term granted (the habendum);

- The recitals (the clause that normally begins "whereas");

- The parcels clause (the clause that normally begins with the words "all that");

- The parties' signatures and the attestation of the witnesses thereto (the modern version of which normally states that the parties have signed the document "as a deed in the presence of" the witnesses).

The same basic structure is followed in relation to a lease except that it also reserves a rent (the *redendum*) and has a number of covenants, conditions and provisos to govern the relationship of landlord and tenant.

Since 1925 deeds executed must be signed. But the present requirement is that a deed must be signed by the parties in the presence of a witness who attests his signature or, where the deed is executed in the presence of one of the parties, the signature must be attested by two witnesses who each attest the signature.[5] The requirement that deeds had to be sealed has now been removed provided the deed states that it is signed as a deed and witnessed.[6]

1.2
The parcels and their construction

The parcels clause is the clause that sets out the land conveyed. It is often crucial of the resolution of boundary disputes. An example from an 1824 conveyance (or indenture) reads as follows:

> "ALL that plot piece or parcel of ground being No 4 in the row of houses situate without St Michael's Road in the suburbs of the City of Muncaster called or known by the name of South Street
>
> AND ALSO ALL that messuage or dwelling house and all and singular other buildings lately erected and built thereon bounded on the South West by the Road fronting the said buildings on the North West by premises belonging to John Parsons being No 3 on the North East by premises belonging to Thomas Fowler and on the south east by premises belonging to Mrs Dugleby being No 5
>
> TOGETHER with all and singular ways rights members and appurtenances to the same respectively belonging".

Some of the language and characteristics of the deed are common to deeds rights up to and after the 1925 property legislation. The words "messuage", often used in earlier deeds, and "house" used in modern ones, both have the effect of passing a dwellinghouse with its curtilage.

---

5 Law Reform (Miscellaneous Provisions) Act 1989 ("LR (MP) A"), section 1(3), replacing section 73 of the Law of Property Act 1925 ("LPA"), which came into force on 31st July 1990.

6 L R (M P) A, section 1(2).

The absence of punctuation will be noted. Punctuation was largely absent in deeds in the past, as it is in deeds today. It will also be noted that a number of archaic words and phrases are used. In deeds of that period it was the practice to describe the parcels in some detail but since 1925 this is less common as, by section 62 of the Law of Property Act 1925, all buildings, erections, fixtures, commons, hedges which appertain or reputedly appertain to the land are conveyed without the need for special mention. The effect of that section may be to extend the amount of land conveyed by virtue of the general words implied into the conveyance.

The title deeds normally constitute the primary source from which the boundary position is established. In cases where the parcels are clear, the existence of a later erroneous description may be disregarded. This will apply where there is a reference in the parcels clause to the physical characteristics of the site (for example, "bounded on or towards the east by the dwellinghouse belonging to John Oglethorpe").[7] In that situation provided the physical description is clear it will take priority, even where measurements are referred to later in the conveyance, for example on a plan. This is on the basis that the Latin maxim *falsa demonstratio non nocet* (a false demonstration does not injure) applies. By that maxim:

> "In construing a deed purporting to assure a property, if there be a description of the property sufficient to render certain what is intended, the addition of a wrong name or erroneous statement as to quantity, occupancy, locality, or an erroneous enumeration of particulars, will have no effect".[8]

Thus in one case the property that the parties intended to convey was described as being in the wrong parish. In other respects the description was correct so that it was held that the incorrect part of the description was rejected and the property was held to pass under the accurate part of the description.[9] But, as *Emmet on Title* points out,[10] where there is a conveyance by reference to general terms followed by specific description, whether by reference to a plan or to a written schedule of particulars, the latter description or plan has the effect of restricting the general description.

---

7   *Eastwood* v *Ashton* [1915] AC 900.
8   *Norton on Deeds* 2nd edition p 214.
9   *Lambe* v *Reaston* (1813) 5 Taunt 207.
10 19th ed. at para 17.010.

It used to be thought that where there are two descriptions of the parcels the first would prevail but the modern view is that it will not matter whether that description is the first or second description of the parcels in the deed provided one of those is clear.[11]

Where there are several descriptions of the parcels none of which is clear there is no particular rule of construction and the court must do its best to make sense of the parties' true intentions.

Strictly the parties' true intentions must be divined from the written instrument and not by oral evidence, for where an agreement is reduced to writing it is necessary to ascertain what is meant by the words used, not what was intended.[12] This rule will certainly apply where the deed is capable of construction but where the deed absents a particular word or phrase the position may be otherwise.[13] Extrinsic evidence may be admitted where the description of the boundaries in the deed is too general, contradictory, uncertain or ambiguous to identify the correct boundary position.[14] In some cases an ambiguity may be resolved from within the deed itself by looking at, for example, recitals and other parts of the deed. In other cases extrinsic evidence may be admitted, for example a grant of planning permission in relation to the property.[15] However, the court will never allow oral evidence to be admitted to contradict the contents of a deed. Such evidence is really limited to evidence which sheds light on the meaning of, and context in which, the deed was executed where an examination of the deed itself does not provide the answer.

The parcels in a conveyance may be described by reference to the name or street number of the property, by its abuttals, by its dimensions, by description of its nature or its inhabitants, or its past and present nature or mode of occupation. The function of the description of the parcels in each case is to indicate clearly which property is to be conveyed with such precision that there is no room for doubt. In order to further that object drafters often include plans. Unfortunately, these have given rise to a number of problems of their own and they will therefore now be considered separately.

---

11 See *Halsbury's Laws* vol 4 (1) 4th ed 2002 reissue at para 928.
12 *Prenn v Simmonds* [1971] 1 WLR 1381. The court is, of course, always concerned to discover the meaning of the words used and it is sometimes necessary to consider what the parties meant by the words they used. What the court cannot do is to admit oral evidence where it contradicts the plain words they have used in a written instrument (see Lewison 'The Interpretation of Contracts' 2nd ed. at para 1–07).
13 *IS Mills (Yardley) Ltd v Curdworth Investments Ltd* (1975) 235 EG 113.
14 *Lyle v Richards* (1866) LR 1 HL 222.
15 See *Murly v M'Dermott* (1838) 8 Ad & El 138.

1.3
The plan and cases where it is inconsistent with the parcels

The parcels are frequently described by reference to a plan and the natural inference in that situation is that the plan would enable the person reading the conveyance to see what land passed by that deed.[16] However, there is often an inconsistency between the description of the parcels and the plan. If the plan is described as being "for identification purposes only" then the description of the parcels will prevail,[17] i.e. the plan is merely an aid to construction. If the property is "more particularly described on the plan" then the plan will prevail over the parcels clause in so far as there is a discrepancy.[18] Where, however, the description of the parcels is inadequate the court may consider the plan in determining what land was intended to be conveyed even though the plan is described as being for "identification purposes only".[19] This will be the case also where the deed does not refer to the plan but there is nevertheless a plan attached.[20] Should the verbal description of the parcels and the plan not agree then in certain cases extrinsic evidence of the factual background against which the contract was entered into may be adduced as an aid to construction[21] but extrinsic evidence will not be admitted to contradict the parcels even where they are only ascertainable from a plan marked "for identification purposes".[22]

It is not unusual for there to be a description of the parcels by reference to a plan marked "for identification purposes" but then the phrase "more particularly delineated on the plan annexed hereto" to appear. In such a case the two phrases effectively cancel each other out.[23] The plan had no predominance over the description in the parcels clause and the court would be unlikely to derive much guidance from it. The court would have to construe the conveyance as best it could.

---

16 *AJ Dunning (Shop fitters) Ltd* v *Sykes and Son (Poole) Ltd* [1987] 1 All ER 700 especially at 706.
17 *Hopgood* v *Brown* [1955] 1 WLR 213, *Neilson* v *Poole* (1969) 20 P & CR 909.
18 *Eastwood* v *Ashton* [1915] AC 900 and see Norton on Deeds 2nd ed.at p.237.
19 *Wigginton & Milner Ltd* v *Winster Engineering Ltd* [1978] 1 WLR 1462, *Targett* v *Ferguson* (1996) 72 P & CR 106.
20 *Leachman* v *Richardson* [1969] 1 WLR 1129.
21 *Scarfe* v *Adams* [1981] 1 All ER 843.
22 See *Woolls* v *Powling, Times* 9/3/99.
23 *Neilson* v *Poole* (1969) 20 P & CR 909,Ch D.

The need for accuracy in preparing a plan is obvious but inaccuracy in a plan will not vitiate a sufficiently certain description of the land conveyed unless the dimensions of the land are an essential part of the description or definition of the land conveyed.[24] It is the duty of the grantor to ensure the accuracy of a plan because a deed is construed *contra proferentum* the grantor. But a plan will rarely be sufficient to define the boundary of a small part of a larger building, particularly where the Ordnance Survey is relied on. The Court of Appeal has said that in such a case each parcel conveyed should be described with particularity and precision.[25] In registered land provision for a parcels clause is made in the standard form of transfer used[26] and it is appropriate to draft this with care, particularly where part of a larger property is to be transferred.

The *falsa demonstratio non nocet maxim*[27] may also apply in relation to plans. Thus where, for example, the description makes it plain that the boundary goes down the centre line of a boundary feature, the fact that the plan shows the boundary line being, say, at the foot of a hedge, will not alter the description of the parcels. In such a case, as the description in the parcels clause is clear, any court construing it will be forced to ignore the plan.[28]

A plan that is "for delineation only" is normally one not drawn to scale. On the other hand words such as "more particularly delineated on" a plan or "more precisely described" on a plan annexed to a conveyance are generally thought to suggest that the plan should prevail in a case of conflict.[29] In some cases the description is so confusing that neither the verbal description nor the plan can be said to take precedence.[30]

Sometimes an Ordnance Survey map will be attached to a conveyance and, as we shall see when we consider registered land, the Ordnance Survey forms the basis for the filed plan in all registered land. In relation to boundary features it is important to note that the line shown on the plan taken from the Ordnance Survey marks the centre line of any hedge, fence or wall. Where the parties have adopted

---

24 *Mellor* v *Walmsley* [1905] 2 Ch 164, CA.
25 *Scarfe* v *Adams* [1981] 1 All ER 843.
26 See Land Registration Act 1925 ("LRA 1925"), section 76 and Ruoff and Roper *'Registered Conveyancing'* para's 4.01–4.22.
27 See page 4 above.
28 See *Maxted* v *Plymouth Corporation* (1957) CLY 243, (1957) 169 EG 427.
29 *AJ Dunning (Shopfitters) Ltd* v *Sykes and Son* [1987] Ch 287 at 289.
30 See *Neilson* v *Poole* (1969) 20 P & CR 909.

the Ordnance Survey plan as the basis for a conveyance or a transfer of registered land it will prevail over other presumptions that might otherwise apply in relation to boundary features such as the hedge and ditch presumption, provided it is clear. Where the parcels or the plan accompanying the conveyance are not clear they will not displace any other presumptions that ordinarily apply.[31]

Where the Ordnance Survey is used as the basis for the plan in rural areas the plan will be based on the Ordnance Survey field numbers and plan numbers. The acreage is taken from the centre of a hedge or ditch and Ordnance Survey practice is to show a feature as being within a particular field by using "f" marks.

"T" marks are used on plans accompanying conveyances to show ownership of a boundary feature such as a wall and may therefore be helpful in determining the boundary position. The "T" should be drawn so that it points towards the land of the person on whose land the feature stands. They would represent persuasive evidence in a boundary dispute that the feature in question was owned by the owner towards whose land the T points.

Less commonly "H" marks appear on a plan. These are intended to show the presence of a party boundary feature, the theory being that the H shows two "T" marks together indicating joint ownership. However, some have expressed the view that they provide less persuasive evidence than "T" marks because of their relative rarity.[32]

Plans also sometimes mark the location of a party wall. Such an indication would probably be held to be an indication of the intention that the feature in question is to be party even in the absence of any such reference in the parcels clause.[33]

---

31 See *Fisher* v *Winch* [1939] 1 KB 666 but see also *Wibberley (Alan) Building* v *Insley* [1999] 1 WLR 894.

32 See Aldridge QC '*Boundaries Walls and Fences*' 8th Ed at p7.

33 See Sara on '*Boundaries and Easements*' 2nd edition at p.97–98.

1.4
Consequences of a mistake as to the land conveyed

Cases may arise where one party to the transaction is genuinely mistaken as to what he was buying. Alternatively, the seller may have acquired the property following a misdescription or misrepresentation. Problems of this type commonly occur in relation to the boundary position. Where this occurs important legal consequences may follow, including the right to rescind. These different concepts need only be touched on here and the reader is referred to the standard contract textbooks for a fuller discussion with reference to the modern authorities.[34]

Where a party is mistaken as to what he was purchasing and this may in some cases result in the contract being declared void. Relief may in certain circumstances be available in the form of a rectification action.[35] If the mistake is unilateral and was not contributed to by the party who was not mistaken, rescission will rarely be granted; the assumption being that the mistaken party has contributed to the mistake by failing to make proper enquiries.[36]

A vendor may bring an action to enforce the contract by order of specific performance where the purchaser fails to complete within the time specified in the contract. If the purchaser says by reply that the property was misdescribed then except in the case of a substantial misdescription, he will not be able to avoid the contract altogether unless he is able to show that it was not innocent.[37] In the case of innocent misdescription which is not substantial the purchaser will normally only be entitled to an abatement of the price rather than to rescission of the contract and the seller may therefore serve a notice to complete.[38]

A misrepresentation, on the other hand, for example, involving an innocent misdescription of the property that did not become a term of the contract, will entitle the purchaser to rescind the contract.[39] Whether

---

34 See *Emmet on Title* at chapters 3–4. The right to respond is considered further in section 1 of chapter 9.
35 *Craddock Bros Ltd v Hunt* [1922] 2 Ch 809.
36 See *Solle v Butcher* [1950] 1 KB 671 per Denning LJ and *Chitty on Contracts* 28th ed. chapter 5, especially at 5–089.
37 *Emmet on Title*, 19th ed. at 4.022.
38 See *Bechal v Kitsford Holdings Limited* [1988] 3 All ER 985.
39 See section 2 (2), which provides a remedy in damages in lieu of rescission where the misrepresentation is innocent whereas before the Act rescission was the only remedy for innocent representation.

it becomes a term of the contract or is merely referred to in negotiations, the misrepresentation must have induced the purchaser to enter the contract in order to be actionable. However, in most cases the right to rescind is governed by the conditions in the contract. For example, the 3rd edition of the National Conditions of Sale provide that rescission may only be claimed where fraud or recklessness had occurred or where there was a substantial difference between the quality of that described and the quality of that conveyed.[40] In all other cases the purchaser is left to his claim in damages and these, where they are awarded under the Misrepresentation Act 1967, will be on the tortious measure.[41]

1.5
The role of oral agreement in establishing the correct boundary position

Although the primary method by which parties may delineate the boundary is within a conveyance or transfer, oral agreement is frequently used as a method of agreeing the boundary between neighbours and such an agreement may be effective provided it does not contradict a legal instrument.[42]

Since 27th September 1989, when section 2 of the Law of Property (Miscellaneous Provisions) Act 1989 came into force, contracts for the sale of land must be in signed writing and should include all the terms which the parties have expressly agreed. Where contracts are exchanged each should be signed.[43] The Act expressly abolished the doctrine of part performance.[44] However, the Act is expressed not to affect the "operation of implied, resulting or constructive trusts"[45] and there is an increasing body of cases where it has been possible to argue that such a trust arises so as to avoid the provisions of the Act.[46]

---

40 Condition 7.1.1.

41 See *Royscott Trust v Rogerson* [1991] 2 QB 297.

42 See *Burns v Morton* [1999] 3 All ER 646.

43 LR (MP) A, section 2(1).

44 By repealing section 40 of the Law of Property Act in Schedule 2 with effect from 27th September 1989.

45 LR (MP) A, section 2(5).

46 See for e.g. *Target Holdings Ltd v Priestley* [2000] 79 P & CR 305 and *Yaxley v Gotts* [2000] Ch 162.

A contract for sale of land that satisfies these formal requirements is not by itself sufficient to fix the boundary position since it is the conveyance in unregistered land and registration in registered land which create the legal estate. However, a contract which includes a draft transfer will commit the vendor to transfer the land on that draft transfer[47] and specific performance may be ordered. In such a case the purchaser may be said to have acquired an equitable fee simple[48] of the property to be transferred.

It is also necessary in this context to consider the important area of proprietary estoppel when considering the legal consequences of an oral agreement in relation to land. Proprietary estoppel has been equated with constructive trusts in a number of recent cases,[49] although it is in truth different.[50] This has enabled parties to avoid section 2 of the 1989 Act[51] because, as the name "proprietary estoppel" suggests, it gives rise to proprietary rights and does not merely provide a defence to an action for ejectment.[52]

An estoppel may be said to arise where A makes a promise or gives an assurance to B who acts to his detriment in reliance on that promise or assurance. Alternatively estoppel arises where A acquiesces in B's exercise of rights over his land. If B has placed reliance on A's silence to his detriment A will be estopped from asserting his strict legal rights.[53] Thus – where one of two adjoining owners acts to his detriment on an assumption as to the correct boundary position which, it subsequently transpires, is erroneous – the other neighbour may be estopped from asserting his strict legal rights. The authorities appear to suggest that where one owner is estopped in this way his successor in title will be similarly estopped.[54]

The principles of estoppel are easier to state than to apply. The courts have repeatedly stressed that the underlying rationale for the modern law

---

47 *Seabreeze Properties Ltd v Haw* [1990] EGCS 114.
48 See *Heshim v Zenab* [1960] AC 316.
49 See especially *Lloyds Bank PLC v Rosset* [1991] 1 AC 107.
50 The lack of a unifying principle in the case law has led Kevin Gray to describe the present state of the law as being an "almost irretrievable shambles" (*'Elements of Land Law'* 3rd Edition at p.750).
51 E.g. in *Yaxley v Gotts* (*supra*).
52 See Snell's *'Principles of Equity'* 30th ed. chapter 39.
53 For a helpful summary of the principles of proprietary estoppel see *Chitty on Contracts* 28th ed. at 3–129 and see *Halsbury's Laws* vol 4(1) 2002 re-issue at para.911. See also *Liverpool Victoria Trustee Company v Taylor* [1982] QB 133, one of the leading cases illustrating the modern approach of applying equitable principles to a broad range of factual situations.
54 See *Hopwood v Brown* [1955] 1 WLR 213 and see also *Brikom Investments Ltd v Carr* 1979] QB 467 especially at 484G–485A.

of estoppel is to prevent one party behaving unconscionably[55] and it will be a relatively rare boundary dispute which may be resolved by applying principles of proprietary estoppel.

---

55 See *Gillett v Holt* [2000] 2 All ER 289.

CHAPTER 2

Documentary and other extrinsic evidence

Documentary and other extrinsic evidence

2.1
Introduction
– the conveyancing background

In this chapter it is necessary to consider the various sources to which reference may be made where the correct boundary position cannot be established simply by referring to the title deeds. As we have seen extrinsic evidence outside the direct documents of title is admissible only where the boundary to a parcel of land is unclear from the conveyance or other documents of title, save in relation to rectification proceedings.[56] Before the types of extrinsic evidence that may be available are considered, it is necessary, particularly in relation to unregistered land, to have some knowledge of conveyancing practice and the process of investigation and searching that takes place before title passes.

In unregistered land the abstract, or epitome, of title is the means by which the prospective purchaser investigates title and ensures that there is a good root of title. The abstract must be delivered within the time specified in the contract.[57] It is the job of the purchaser's solicitor to check that the documents attached to the abstract support a good root of title.

There is no statutory definition of a "good root of title" but it has been defined as:

> "An instrument of disposition dealing with or proving on the face of it, without the aid of extrinsic evidence, the ownership of the whole legal and equitable estate in the property sold, containing a description by which the property can be identified and showing nothing to cast any doubt on the title of the disposing party".[58]

---

56 See *Scarfe v Adams* [1981] 1 All ER 843.
57 See clause 4.1.2 of the National Conditions of Sale (23rd ed.), which provides for the delivery of evidence of title immediately on making the contract.
58 *Williams on Vendor and Purchaser* 4th edition at p.124.

It is also relevant to note that where land is unregistered the Land Charges Register may reveal a pending land action or claim in relation to the land to be conveyed. Petitions for bankruptcy are also included in the Land Charges Register.

In registered land the seller is only required to produce copies or abstracts of the documents noted on the register.[59]

Having investigated title the prospective purchaser then raises inquiries before contract and, where necessary, requisitions on title in order to seek clarification of any adverse encumbrances on the title. The seller first completes a property information form. That document is prepared under the Law Society's National Conveyancing Protocol (the current edition "TransAction" was issued in May 2001). It consists of two parts, one to be completed by the seller's solicitor and the other part to be completed by the seller himself. It contains a reference to the boundaries of the property and any dispute that arises from those boundaries.

Where the preliminary inquiries are inadequate in some way the purchaser will seek clarification by issuing requisitions on title. They are intended to resolve any doubt left by perusal of the abstract, and are therefore particularly relevant where the land is unregistered. The seller then sends out a draft contract for consideration and, where necessary, amendment.

Under the scheme introduced with the Protocol it is for the seller to deal with the basic inquiries that arise in almost every case and it for the buyer to then raise any additional enquiries that are relevant to the particular property. These will usually be raised when the draft contract has been studied.

Finally, a conveyance in unregistered land or transfer in registered land is prepared. A new legal estate is created by the conveyance in unregistered land. Where the land is registered, the legal estate comes into existence when the new proprietor's name is entered as the proprietor on the proprietorship register.[60]

---

59 LRA 1925, section 110 (1), but the present requirements are likely to be to be simplified when the new Land Registration Rules are introduced under the Land Registration Act 2002 (see schedule 10, paragraph 2).
60 See LRA 1925, section 123A (5).

2.2
Abstracts of title, deeds and documentary evidence

An abstract consists of an epitome, or summary, of the various documents by which title is deduced as well as a recital of the relevant events that help to indicate how that title was acquired. Thus births, deaths and marriages will be set out. It is by this means that the conveyancer checks that his client is to acquire a good title. For the litigator the abstract frequently assists in drawing up a root of title and ascertaining which are the relevant documents from the point of view of disclosure and preparation for trial. The abstract will be the normal starting position for establishing the relevant and operative conveyance in relation to the land in dispute.

Other deeds such as mortgages, assents to vesting, auction sale particulars, deeds of release and memoranda which dispose of part of the land in question may be helpful in determining the boundary position because they may contain a description of the parcels or a plan of the land which is intended to be conveyed. These documents are tangential to the direct documents of title and are thus, strictly speaking, inadmissible in establishing title.[61] Nevertheless, they may be an aid to construction of those direct documents and sometimes represent important pieces of evidence.

Particulars of sale at an auction at which the property was sold have been admitted as evidence of the correct boundary position where the subsequent conveyance was ambiguous.[62] It is likely that an estate agent's particulars would similarly be admitted as an aid to construction. Such evidence has been admitted to demonstrate the correct boundary of a several fishery adjoining a river to rebut the *ad medium* presumption which applies in relation to non-tidal rivers.[63]

It is also possible for local histories to give some indication of the location or presence of a disputed boundary feature, but these cases are likely to be very rare.

---

61 See *Prenn* v *Simmonds* [1971] 1 WLR 1381, see also *Chitty on Contracts* 28th ed. at 12–094 et seq. This subject is also dealt with in chapter 1.
62 See *Scarfe* v *Adams* [1981] 1 All ER 843, CA.
63 *Ecroyd* v *Coulthard* [1897] 2 Ch 554.

2.3
Contracts

In every conveyance or transfer of freehold land for which a lump sum is paid a contract will be prepared. It is prepared well in advance of the conveyance or transfer. It will make provision for the payment of the deposit and the payment of interest on late completion as well as a range of other things. In particular it will also, in unregistered land, make provision for the delivery of the abstract.[64]

There seems little doubt that where there is a difference between the contract and the conveyance or transfer examining the former may help to illuminate the way that difference arose and thus will be admissible. Draft contracts and the discussions and negotiations that precede them will rarely be admissible even as an aid to construction because the parol evidence rule excludes reference to anything other than the written contract itself.[65] Extrinsic documents such as sale particulars and preliminary replies before contact may be an aid to construction and help clarify any ambiguity. But, needless to say the contract itself, where it is clear, will rank higher than any pre-contractual documents such as the inquiries before contract.

---

64 In registered land the seller provides the information referred to in section 110 of the Land Registration Act 1925 (the equivalent provision is in schedule 10, para. 2 of the Land Registration Act 2002).

65 *Chitty on Contracts* 28th ed. at paragraph 12–094.

2.4
Documents relating to boundaries fixed under miscellaneous statutory and other powers

Under the Inclosure Act 1845 there was the power to make orders fixing boundaries and where such an order has been made it may provide historical evidence of the boundary position.

In relation to common land there is now a complicated and little understood system of registration under the Commons Registration Act 1965. The register provides authoritative evidence of the boundaries of the common.[66]

It appears that a court of equity has power to set up a commission of inquiry into a boundary position[67] but this power would not be exercised merely because there is some confusion as to the correct boundary position. There must have been some inequitable conduct so as to found the court's equitable jurisdiction and they are extremely rare in modern times.

2.5
Statutory declarations

The purpose of a statutory declaration is to substitute the evidence of a person with knowledge of the title in question for the documents of title. This may be because those documents of title have been lost or are missing or because title to the land in question is based on adverse possession. Their form and content is governed by the Statutory Declarations Act 1835. They generally provide proof of ownership sufficient to satisfy a prospective purchaser of the land in question. Since the Civil Evidence Act 1968 statutory declarations have been admissible in civil proceedings[68] provided the necessary notices are served.[69] They are frequently accepted by HM Land Registry and are often submitted in support of claims to registration.

---

66 Commons Registration (General) Regulations 1966 SI 1966/1471.
67 *Searle* v *Cooke* (1890) 43 Ch D 519 at 527, CA.
68 They would now be admitted under section 2 of the Civil Evidence Act 1995.
69 Now governed by CPR Part 33.2.

2.6
Maps

Since 1841 the Ordnance Survey have provided detailed mapping of England and Wales. As well as forming the basis for the filed plans in registered land[70] Ordnance Survey maps, which are available in a variety of scales, are often helpful in identifying the property and resolving ambiguity relating to the correct boundary position.[71]

Private boundaries may also be marked on maps prepared from inclosure awards. Although they will not generally be entirely accurate, they may nevertheless assist where there is other evidence of the correct boundary position. They may mark such things as the position of a nearby highway.

Maps, dating from the nineteenth century and earlier, which established liability for payment of tithes are generally thought to be reasonably accurate and are therefore sometimes helpful in resolving boundary disputes. It was provided by the Tithe Act 1864 that any plan annexed to an instrument of tithe apportionment was to be deemed satisfactory evidence of the accuracy of such a plan. But, in order to be admissible the map must have been prepared by a person under a duty to record the relevant facts for the purposes of making them publicly available[72] and these maps were not intended to provide evidence of the boundary between two adjoining properties.[73] They may nevertheless be of some assistance in ascertaining that position.

Finally, in relation to land adjoining a highway, turnpike maps may still sometimes be located which help to indicate the boundary of the relevant parcel of land.

---

70 An office copy of which is admissible as if it were the original (LRA 1925, s.113).

71 But, where the Ordnance Survey is used for the filed plan in registered land it is Land Registry practice to mark boundary features with a single line marking the midway point unless the parties require the boundary you be fixed.

72 See *Giffard* v *Williams* (1890) 38 LJ Ch 597.

73 *Wilberforce* v *Hearfield* (1877) 5 Ch D 709.

2.7
Photographs and other
miscellaneous evidence

Where extrinsic evidence is admissible it may take the form of photographs,[74] which are often of greater assistance to a court in resolving a boundary dispute than the oral evidence of witnesses, who may often be mistaken as to the correct boundary position or downright dishonest. Nevertheless, witnesses are often called to resolve boundary disputes and sometimes provide the only evidence available.[75]

Extrinsic evidence may take the form of a grant of planning consent in relation to disputed land. Public documents of that type may be used as evidence of the facts upon which they are based.[76]

Evidence of general reputation is only admissible where it relates to a matter of general or public interest, for example the boundary of a parish[77] or town.[78] Thus it would only be in a case where the parish or town boundary is said to coincide with a private boundary that such a document would be relevant.

As we have seen[79] evidence in a tithe map has been admitted on the basis that the person preparing it must have intended to record the relevant facts and have intended to make the statement publicly available.[80]

Evidence of reputation or family tradition relevant to any matter before court may also be admitted for the purpose of proving any public or general right.[81]

It has also been held that the verdict of a judge or jury in an earlier case may be admitted as evidence of the boundary position.[82] Where such evidence is admissible it may be given orally or in documentary form, provided the other rules of evidence are complied with.

---

74 The admission of these is now governed by CPR 33.6.
75 See section 2.8 below.
76 Civil Evidence Act 1995, section 9.
77 *R* v *Mytton* (1860) 2 E & E 557.
78 *Ireland* v *Powell* (1802) 7 Ad & El at 555.
79 On page 19.
80 See *Giffard* v *Williams* (1869) 38 LJ Ch 597 at 604.
81 Provided the procedure set out in the Civil Evidence Act 1995 (CEA) and the rules made there under (see CPR Part 33) are followed.
82 *Evans* v *Rees* (1839) 10 Ad REL 151.

There is also provision in the current rules for the admission of video evidence and even models in court proceedings but these are rarely used in practice.[83]

2.8
Witnesses

The recollections of witnesses, sometimes going back over many years, will sometimes constitute the only evidence available to resolve a boundary dispute. Mutual exchange of witness statements has been permitted by the rules of procedure governing the county courts and High Court since the mid 1980's and it is now a requirement of the Civil Procedure Rules 1998 (CPR) that witness statements should be in prescribed form and disclosed with the claimant's claim form where the claim is under CPR Part 8. Part 8 applies if there is no dispute of fact or the claim is one that must be brought using the procedure set out in that rule.[84] The defendant should serve its witness statements with its acknowledgement of service in such a case. In cases to which Part 7 of the CPR applies (the bulk of claims) the court will fix a date for witness statements to be served and the order in which that is to be done.[85]

Under the Civil Evidence Act 1995, which applies to all civil proceedings commenced after 31st January 1997, no evidence is to be excluded merely on the grounds that it is hearsay.[86] However, as under the Civil Evidence Act 1968, there is provision within the CPR[87] for the service of notice on the other side before such evidence is used.

A statement in a document is no longer to be excluded on the grounds that it contains hearsay[88] and producing the original or an authenticated copy may prove that document.[89] There is also provision in the CPR for witnesses to give evidence by video link and courts are likely to be sympathetic to a request to adduce evidence in that way provided facilities are available.[90]

---

83 See CPR 33.6.
84 CPR 8.5 and 32.
85 CPR 32.4.
86 CEA 1995, section 2.
87 CPR 33.2.
88 CEA 1995, section 1(1).
89 CEA 1995, section 4.
90 CPR 32.3. Most larger courts have video conference facilities which are, generally, under used. These can be used for shorter hearings as well as for witnesses who are unable to attend court.

However, the normal rule remains that witnesses should attend trial in person to give their evidence[91] and a party intending to rely on hearsay evidence should give notice of his intention to do so specifying a reason for not calling that witness.[92] Where evidence is admitted under the 1995 Act the court is to have regard to various matters in judging the weight to attach to that evidence including whether it would have been reasonable and practicable for that witness to give evidence.[93]

---

91 CPR 32. 2(1)(a).
92 CEA 1995, section 2.
93 CEA 1995, section 4.

The physical evidence on site

The physical evidence on site

3.1
Boundary features

Boundary features such as hedges, fences and walls although seemingly substantial on the ground are usually shown by the Ordnance Survey (the basis for most modern plans) by a single line. That line will be drawn down the centre of the boundary feature. More substantial features such as tracks may be shown by a double line or lines.

Where a particular physical feature is said to represent the boundary position it is necessary to identify whether the extremity of that feature or whether the median line represents the correct boundary position. It may be easier to determine the median line of a recently constructed wall than an ancient hedge. Even where a fixed object such as the face of a wall forms the boundary it may be practically difficult to determine the precise position of the boundary in places: where, for example, that wall bows.

Where the boundary feature is a structure there may also be questions as to the extent to which the foundations may extend beyond the strict boundary line represented by its vertical face above the ground.[94] Strictly speaking such foundations as well as drain pipes, spouts and other rainwater goods may trespass over the boundary where a building is constructed right up to the boundary line. But in practice it seems rare for the owner of land to argue with rights to use the sub-soil deep below his property and clearly after the appropriate period the rights of the paper title owner to that land may be extinguished.

Some of the problems that previously arose in relation to access to neighbouring land have now been resolved by the Access to Neighbouring

---

94 There is no automatic right at common law to enter a neighbour's land even where building operations are necessary for the maintenance of a property but there is now a power for a court to order access under the Access to Neighbouring Land Act 1992 (see section 6.4 of chapter 6).

Land Act 1992.[95] Under section 1 of that Act where the owner of the neighbouring land does not consent to access by his neighbour, that neighbour may apply to the county court for an access order. An access order will be granted for the purposes of carrying out maintenance and repair work provided the work is reasonably necessary.[96]

3.2
Horizontal and vertical boundaries

The Law of Property Act 1925[97] recognises that a boundary may be "horizontal vertical or made in any other way".

Theoretically a vertical boundary extends to the subsoil beneath the boundary to the centre of the earth[98] and extends up to the sky above.[99] Thus it has been held that the owner of land in London's Docklands could enjoin the erection of cranes placed in order to carry out above its land construction work[1] on adjacent land even though it could not be shown that there was a substantial interference with the claimant's enjoyment of its land. But the owner of a country residence could not enjoin the flying of aircraft over his property on the grounds that it was a trespass.[2] The purpose of the law of trespass is to prevent unlawful interference with the enjoyment of one's land and the true rationale of many of the cases seems to be to prevent the interference with the claimant's existing or potential use of his land. The erection of cranes, albeit for a temporary duration, appears to fall within this category.[3]

In addition to the vertical boundary it is frequently necessary to determine a horizontal boundary. Any feature may be said to mark a horizontal boundary. However, in practice the position is often more complex and particular problems may be encountered in relation to

---

95 The Act will be fully considered in section 6.4 of chapter 6.
96 Section 1(2).
97 Section 205(ix).
98 *Duke of Devonshire* v *Pattinson* (1887) 20 QBD 263.
99 See *Corbett* v *Hill* (1870) LR 9 Eq 671.
1 *Anchor Brewhouse Limited* v *Berkley House (Docklands Developments) Limited* [1987] 2 EGLR 173 and see *Kelsen* v *Imperial Tobacco* [1957] 2 QB 334, which involved the erection of advertising hoardings.
2 *Bernstein* v *Skyviews & General* [1978] QB 479, but the occupation of the airspace in this way may constitute a nuisance in some cases.
3 In practice a landowner is unlikely to be able to take objection to any thing carried out more than 200 yards above an existing building on his land.

mineral rights, which exist below ground level, or in relation to a flying freehold. Difficult questions arise as to the precise position of, for example, a horizontal boundary under a passageway; is it marked by the floor of that passageway or by ceiling of a room below that floor?

The starting position is to ascertain the words of grant in the lease or conveyance, if necessary, with the assistance of the recitals.[4] A lease or conveyance is generally to be construed by reference to the conditions existing at the date of grant.[5]

Basements of premises adjoining streets that are built under the street extend up to the horizontal boundary between the highway and the sub-soil. Where there is a basement extending beneath such a highway the Land Registry will, in appropriate cases, be prepared to register it and mark it on the filed plan. Even where they are not so marked they pass on a disposition of registered land under rule 251 of the Land Registration Rules.[6]

Where land is held on leasehold tenure the external walls enclosing the demised premises form part of those demised premises unless the lease provides to the contrary.[7] A covenant that the landlord is to carry out external repairs does not alter that presumption.[8] Where a lease of a flat includes the roofspace and roof above the demise it will extend to the airspace above the roof and, sometimes to the roof above an adjacent flat unless it is expressly excluded.[9] A demise of particular floor of a building will include the voids in a false ceiling above.[10] The lessee may only use the walls to the demised premises and may not trespass on the property of an adjoining owner, however.

---

4   See *Doe'd White* v *Osborne* (1840) 4 Jur 941, (1840) 9 LCJP 313.
5   See Hill and Redman '*Law of Landlord and Tenant*' at A 1526.
6   Which provides that registration vests appurtenances that appertain to the land in the registered proprietor.
7   *Sturge* v *Hackett* [1962] 1 WLR 1257.
8   See *Campden Hill Towers Limited* v *Gardner* [1977] QB 823.
9   See *Davies* v *Yadegar* [1990] 1 EGLR 71 and *Hatfield* v *Moss* [1988] 2 EGLR 58.
10 *Graystone Property Investments Ltd* v *Margulies* (1983) 47 P & CR 472.

3.3
Inferences and presumptions

In some cases ownership of a boundary feature will be obvious even in the absence of express provision in the documents of title. An artificial structure such as a wall or fence in the absence of provision to the contrary belongs to the owner on whose land it stands. If on the true construction of the documents of title it is not possible to establish who owns a particular feature then it may be necessary to have regard to certain established presumptions, which apply in relation to some boundary features. The presumptions which are referred to below are rebuttable, in that evidence to rebut them is always admissible but until that evidence is produced the presumptions continue to apply.[11]

There is a presumption that where land is conveyed adjoining a highway or road[12] the conveyance operates to transfer ownership of the sub-soil up to the middle of that highway or road.[13] But this presumption will be displaced by the wording of the conveyance which contradicts that presumption.[14]

However, in relation to adopted highways it is Land Registry practice to show the frontage of the land adjoining the highway as marking the boundary whatever the ownership of the subsoil of the highway itself.

The presumption that applies in relation to land which adjoins a highway does not apply in relation to land which adjoins a railway so that the owner of land that adjoins a railway will not have the right to extract minerals that lie beneath that track.[15]

There is also a presumption that where a structure built up to the boundary line requires support by means, for example, of a buttress or, in the case of a fence, by a supporting upright member, those buttresses or members project onto the land of the owner of the structure. Thus the boundary line will generally be at the extremity of the structural support not the structure itself.

---

11 *Fisher* v *Winch* [1939] 1 KB 666.
12 This presumption is more fully considered in section 1 of chapter 7.
13 *Berridge* v *Ward* (1861) 10 CB (NS) 400, see also *Emmet on Title* 19th ed. para.17.025.
14 *Giles* v *County Building Constructors Ltd* (1971) 22 P & CR 978.
15 *Thompson* v *Hickman* [1907] 1 Ch 550 and a conveyance under section 77 of the Railway Clauses Consolidation Act 1845 does not pass the minerals beneath unless they are expressly included in that conveyance, i.e. otherwise they are retained by the vendor (see chapter 8).

Local custom may also be evidence of the way boundary features are constructed and who they are intended to be owned by. In *Collis* v *Amphlett*[16] a fence had been erected on land that adjoined a common but was placed four feet from the apparent boundary line. It was alleged that this was normal practice and although that argument was rejected on the facts, the court was prepared to hear evidence of the local custom.

3.4
The hedge and ditch presumption

This provides that where a hedge and ditch are found along a boundary between two parcels of land it is presumed that the boundary between the two properties lies at the far side of the ditch and not at the edge or down the centre line of the hedge. It is presumed that ownership of a ditch in dispute lies with the owner whose land lies on the side where the hedge has grown because it is assumed that the hedge grew upon soil excavated from the ditch at the far side of the hedge[17] (which it is assumed was thrown onto the owner's own land) unless it can be shown that the ditch was in place when the boundary was drawn.[18] As Lord Hoffman has explained[19] this is because the hedge and ditch rule involves the presumption that the ditch was dug after the boundary was drawn in order to mark the boundary. Where there was evidence to the contrary the presumption would be rebutted. Thus if the hedge has been there longer than the ditch the presumption cannot apply.

But, it appears, the presumption can only be rebutted by the strong evidence that the boundary was drawn after the hedge was planted, as occurred in the case of *Falkingham* v *Farley*.[20] In that case there was a carefully prepared plan executed for the purpose of an auction of the land in 1914, which showed the boundary running through the hedge and not at the far side of the ditch.

The presumption is not rebutted by evidence of possession by the adjoining owner, for example tending the hedge or cleaning the ditch,

---

16 [1918] 1 Ch 232.
17 *Vowels* v *Miller* (1810) 3 Taunt 137 at 138.
18 *Alan Wibberley Building Limited* v *Insley HL* [1999] 1 WLR 894.
19 In *Alan Wibberley Building Limited* v *Insley HL* [1999] 1 WLR 894.
20 (CA) *Times*, March 11, 1991.

even if these have continued for many years.[21] But there is nothing to prevent a squatter claiming title by adverse possession to the land up to the hedge, for example where the ditch has been filled in.[22] On the other hand where there have been joint acts of ownership on both sides of the hedge it may be possible to establish that the hedge is in fact a party hedge.

The presumption does not apply where the ditch is natural rather than artificial because the intentions of the original owner, in planting a hedge, cannot be assumed in the way that they are where the hedge and ditch rule applies.[23] Nor will the presumption apply where the title deeds show where the boundary is[24] or where there are two ditches one each side of the hedge. In the latter situation it will be necessary to look to the acts of ownership of each neighbour to ascertain ownership of the boundary. The rule will not be defeated by the sale of land purporting to belong to the seller, but which, according to the rule, belongs to his neighbour.[25]

The hedge and ditch rule conflicts with Land Registry practice, which is to show the centre line of the hedge as representing the boundary but as we shall see this is said to represent the general boundary only and thus may be rebutted by the hedge and ditch rule. The hedge and ditch rule will not apply, however, where the land is conveyed or transferred by express reference to the Ordnance Survey plan.[26]

21 *Henniker* v *Howard* (1904) 90 LT 157.
22 See *Marshall* v *Taylor* [1895] 1 Ch. 641.
23 *Marshall* v *Taylor* supra.
24 *Fisher* v *Winch* [1939] 1 KB 666.
25 *Hall* v *Dorling* [1996] EGCS 58.
26 *Rouse* v *Gravel Works Ltd* [1940] 1 KB 489.

CHAPTER 4
Boundaries of registered land

Boundaries of registered land

4.1
Introduction to the system of land registration

The system of land registration introduced by the Land Registration Act 1925 represented a new development of the law. There is a fundamental difference between registered and unregistered land in that title must be investigated afresh on every conveyance of unregistered land whereas the prospective purchaser is entitled to assume the register is correct where he is purchasing registered land. In theory the state guarantees title so the onus is no longer on the purchaser to ensure that good title to all the land intended to be conveyed is established.

In unregistered land the purchaser or purchaser's solicitor must investigate title by obtaining and studying an abstract or epitome of title to ensure that it supports a good root of title. In registered land the seller needs only to provide a copy of the subsisting entries on the register, a copy of the filed plan and copies or abstracts of documents noted on the register.[27] Under section 110(4) of the Land Registration Act 1925 the register is conclusive in relation to abstracts and excerpts of documents referred to in it.[28]

The state's guarantee of title to registered land means that any loss that flows from a failure of the register to show accurately the encumbrances that there are on the title is subject to a right to compensation. However, there are important limitations on this

---

27 Land Registration Act 1925, section 110 (1), but the Land Registration Act 2002 enables the Lord Chancellor to introduce less onerous requirements under the rules which are to be introduced under schedule 10, paragraph 2 of that Act.
28 Section 120 of the Land Registration Act 2002 contains similar provisions whereby documents kept by the Registrar are conclusive.

indemnity principle which are worth mentioning here, for example, overriding interests are not shown on the register and thus there is no right to an indemnity when they are not discovered. A legal easement constitutes an overriding interest and therefore may not appear on the register. Overiding interests, especially the right of actual occupation, have given rise to a number of difficulties in practice.[29]

Since 1988, the register has been a public record available to anyone prepared to pay the fee[30] and, since 1997, registration has been compulsory on completion of a sale in England and Wales.[31] At present nearly all urban areas are registered and every new conveyance of unregistered land will result in first registration.[32]

As we have seen,[33] There are important differences between land registration practice and the practice in relation to unregistered land.[34] These differences are likely to be exacerbated by the introduction of paperless transactions, promised by HM Land Registry in its annual report for 1999–2000 and expected to be introduced shortly.[35]

The introduction of compulsory electronic conveyancing is facilitated by section 93 of the Land Registration Act 2002. It is likely to require a lengthy period of consultation and the model to be adopted has not yet been agreed. However, the scope for confusion as to the precise boundary position may, if anything, be increased by the adoption of electronic means to transfer title.

In addition to paperless conveyancing the Land Registration Act 2002[36] introduces some important changes to the land registration system. Although it received Royal Assent on 26th February 2002 it will not become law until the Lord Chancellor fixes a date. There will need to be a new set of Land Registration Rules approved by Parliament

---

29 See *Williams and Glyns Bank Limited* v *Boland* [1981] AC 487.

30 Land Registration Act 1988, which commenced on 3rd December 1990.

31 Land Registration Act 1997.

32 Land Registration Act 1925, section 123A added by the Land Registration Act 1997, but the number of triggers to first registration will be increased by section 4 of the Land Registration Act 2002.

33 In chapter 2.

34 See generally Megarry and Wade '*The Law of Real Property*' 6th ed. chapter 6.

35 The Electronic Communications Act 2000, by section 8, allows a minister to carry out by order any change or modification to existing legislation to facilitate electronic communication and as we shall see there are also provisions in Part 8 and Schedule 5 of the Land Registration Act 2002 to enable dispositions of registered land to be made and registered electronically simultaneously. Although the power to introduce e-conveyancing is now on the statute books and is supposed to be imminent, in practice there may be some way to go (see *Law Society Gazette* 22/3/01and also '*Land Registration for the 21 Century*' Law Commission 254 (September 1998)).

36 For a helpful guide to the new Act see Harpum and Bignell '*The Land Registration Act 2002*'.

before this can be done so that it is unlikely that the new Act will come into force before the autumn of 2003. Some of the more important changes that will impact on the subject matter of this publication are:

- The disappearance of cautions and inhibitions against first dealings (there will be a new system of cautions against first registration recorded in an index of such cautions).[37]

- Changes in the system of registering cautions whereby owners of land will no longer be able to register a caution over their own land but will have instead to substantively register their title (one of the aims of the new Act is to encourage this).

- The complete reform of the law of adverse possession (this is dealt with in the next chapter).

- The creation of a new office of adjudicator to deal with certain types of registration disputes (intended to be an inexpensive and speedy way of resolving disputes that arise out of applications for registration).

4.2
The general boundaries rule

The Ordnance Survey, which forms the basis for the plan filed with registered land, shows only the general boundary of the property registered.[38] Unless the parties apply to fix the boundary under rule 276 of the Land Registration Rules 1925[39] the filed plan will only show by way of general identification the existing or historic topographic features and give some indication of the position of the boundary, the exact whereabouts of which has been left "undetermined".[40] Where there is no physical boundary in existence the fullest possible particulars of the boundary position must be added to the plan.[41] But the boundary may be revised, or corrected on written application of the proprietor to the

---

37 Land Registration Act 2002, section 60(1)(c).
38 Land Registration Rules 1925 ("LRR"), rule 278.
39 The Land Registration Act 2002 contains a similar power under section 60.
40 The general boundaries rule is preserved in section 60 of the 2002 Act, which provides that it applies unless the parties apply to have the boundary fixed.
41 LRR, rule 279 (as amended).

Registrar. The Registrar may require the production of such evidence and the giving of such notice, as he deems necessary[42] and he has the power to determine any discrepancy between the verbal particulars of the land in question and the filed plan or general map.[43]

It is anticipated under the Land Registration Act 2002 greater use will be made of the power in section 60 of that Act to apply to the Registrar for him to fix the exact line of the boundary.

The rule is reflected in the Standard Conditions of Sale,[44] which provide[45] that the seller is absolved from proving the exact boundaries and position of fences, hedges, walls etc. But the purchaser may insist that the seller provides a statutory declaration as to the ownership of those boundaries.

But it is appropriate to be cautious when considering the Ordnance Survey plan, particularly when it is the only evidence as to the correct boundary position. As Peter Gibson LJ said in *Hambrook v Fox*:[46]

> "Caution may be appropriate when one looks at an Ordnance Survey plan or a Land Registry plan, which is of course taken from the last ordnance survey plan for the area. In relation to a hedge, it may be that the plan does not assist in determining whether that is or is not the boundary between the two properties. One must always look at features on the ground. But in my judgement it would be going too far to say that no help at all is obtainable from such plans and in particular from Land Registry plans".

The Land Registry plan does not provide conclusive evidence of ownership in relation to any adjoining feature, such as a road or stream, even if that feature is referred to in the title. But where there is an express agreement in relation to that feature it is possible for the owner to apply to the Registrar for that agreement to be entered on the register.[47]

The more precise ascertainment of the correct boundary position may have to be arrived at by applying one of the rebutable presumptions referred to elsewhere in this work, for example by applying the hedge and ditch rule or the midway rule in relation to land adjoining highways and non-tidal rivers. Where none of those presumptions apply or on the

---

42 LRR, rule 284.
43 LRR, rule 285.
44 3rd edition.
45 In condition 4.3.1.
46 February 8th 1993, unreported.
47 LRA 1925, section 76.

facts a presumption is rebutted by the evidence, the boundary has to be determined by reference to the topographical features and, if necessary, the other evidence as it is in relation to unregistered land.

It is the practice of the Land Registrar to apply the presumptions which apply to unregistered land so that unless a boundary feature is expressly incorporated into one owner's title the Land Registry will assume that ownership of it remains in doubt. Such uncertainty is, however, likely to be relatively rare.

4.3
Categories of title-absolute, possessory and qualified

Although, in theory, the state guarantees title, there are different grades of title.[48] This grading system is supposed to assist the purchaser in establishing the extent of the risk involved in acquiring the land in question.

Absolute title

If "absolute title" is awarded, the registrar is satisfied that the applicant for first registration has good title, which is unlikely to be disturbed. Save in relation to overriding interests the owner in possession of land with absolute title will only be subject to rectification in "exceptional circumstances".[49] However the fact that even absolute title may be interrupted shows that title to registered land is not, as it was intended to be,[50] indefeasible.[51]

---

48 The categories of title are not changed by the Land Registration Act 2002 (see sections 9–10 of that Act).
49 LRA 1925, section 82 (3), but under the Land Registration Act 2002 the court may not order rectification so as to affect the title of a registered proprietor in relation to land in his possession (Land Registration Act 2002 schedule 4).
50 LRA 1925, section 5.
51 See Kevin Gray *'Elements of Land Law'* 3rd ed at p. 237.

Possessory title

The second category of freehold title capable of registration is possessory title. This category will be awarded where the applicant for first registration is unable to prove absolute title by producing adequate documentary evidence in support of his claim to title. If, subsequently, the registered proprietor is able to show that he has been in possession of the land for twelve years without interruption the Registrar must, on an application being made, convert title into absolute title provided he is "satisfied" as to that title.[52]

The practice of the Land Registry where title to land is disputed is to register possessory title only. But the registration of possessory title does not necessarily mean that the Land Registry accept that the title is legitimate, merely that there is a claim to possessory title or paper title that may be disputed which must be resolved by consent or by the courts. Alternatively, the Land Registry is indicating that adequate documentary evidence has not been provided in support of the claim to title absolute.

Once any boundary dispute has been resolved the Land Registry will normally register title absolute in favour of the successful party.

Qualified title

In rare cases the Registrar may grant qualified title, by which is meant title that appears to him to contain flaws. It may be, for example, that there is an estate or interest, which it appears may constitute a defect in the particular title but is not sufficiently clear for the Land Registrar to register a contrary title. The qualification may also arise out the fact that a title may be granted due to some earlier instrument for a limited period only. Once he is satisfied that those flaws have been rectified the Registrar will convert title into absolute title.[53]

---

52 LRA 1925, section 77 (2) and LRR, rule 48 (2).
53 LRA 1925, section 77 but under the Land Registration Act 2002 a number of people may apply for the title to be upgraded and the effect of upgrading is stated with greater precision (see sections 62–63).

4.4
Rectification of the register and the indemnity principle

Rectification of the register may be ordered where one of the grounds in section 82 of the Land Registration Act 1925 ("LRA 1925") exist.[54] Section 82 of the LRA 1925 gives the court or the Registrar the power to rectify the register where:

(a) A court has decided that any person is entitled to any estate, right or interest in or to any registered land.

(b) A court on an application by a person "aggrieved by an entry on the register" makes an order for rectification.

(c) The parties have consented to the rectification concerned.

(d) A court or the Registrar is satisfied that any entry on the register has been obtained by fraud.

(e) Two or more persons are registered by mistake as the proprietors of any registered estate or charge.

(f) A mortgagee has been registered as a proprietor of the land as opposed to a proprietor of a charge and the right to redemption is subsisting.

(g) The legal estate has been registered in the name of a person who, if the land had not been registered would not have been the estate owner.

(h) In any other circumstance where it is considered just and equitable to rectify the register.

The Registrar also has the power to rectify the register where registration is made in error under rule 14 of the Land Registration Rules 1925. However, that power may only be exercised where the parties consent or, where a dispute has arisen, when the court has already reached a decision.

---

54 Under the Land Registration Act 2002 references to "rectification" in relation to the Register shall refer to alterations which involve the correction of a mistake which prejudicially affect the title of a registered proprietor (Schedule 4) and rectification is only one form of alteration of the Register.

It should be noted that rectification on grounds of fraud would only be made where the fraud relates to the obtaining of the entry on the register as opposed to the original disposal of land or an interest in land.[55]

The ground most frequently of importance to the practitioner when dealing with boundary disputes is 82 (1) (g), which enables the register to be rectified where the wrong proprietor has been registered.

The discretion under section 82 (1) (h) (the just and equitable ground) is available on a broad basis. In *Norwich and Peterborough Building Society* v *Steed (No 2)*[56] Scott LJ held that the purpose of the sub-section was to provide a catch-all provision for cases not covered by any of the other categories above. However, the building society in that case could not have a charge removed from the Register because it had not been registered as a result of an "error or omission" and had not been made under a "mistake". The defendant no longer alleged fraud or *non est factum* and the case did not fall within the catch all "just and equitable" category since the transfer that was impugned by the building society was valid at the time when the building society advanced its mortgage money and had been validly registered. Rectification was not an appropriate remedy therefore.

The effect of rectification is not retrospective. Thus it may not affect a lease granted in ignorance of a defect in title, which was wrongly omitted at the time of first registration.[57] Secondly, the Registrar's power to rectify the Register may not provide a complete solution to the problem that frequently arises, for example as to the correct construction of a deed. In such a situation it would be open to the court to reach a different view of the meaning of the deed than the Land Registrar.

There will be a wider power to "alter" the Register under the Land Registration Act 2002. It will also be possible to alter the new Register of Cautions which that Act creates.[58] The new Act is designed to make the process of alteration more transparent and intelligible.[59] Rectification under Schedule 4 of the new Act will be one form of alteration which involves the correction of a mistake that prejudicially affects the title of a registered proprietor. Under the new Act the only case in which rectification will be ordered so as to affect the title of a registered proprietor without his consent will be where there has been

---

55 *Norwich and Peterborough Building Society* v *Steed (No. 2)* [1993] Ch 116.
56 *Supra.*
57 *Freer* v *Unwins* [1976] Ch. 288.
58 Land Registration Act 2002, section 19.
59 Land Registration Act 2002, schedule 4.

fraud or lack of proper care by the registered proprietor or it would be unjust not to make the alteration in the register that is sought.[60]

---

60 Land Registration Act 2002, schedule 4, para 3(2).

CHAPTER 5
Extinction of title

Extinction of title

5.1
The requirements for and effect of a successful adverse possession claim

"No action may be brought by any person for the recovery of land after the expiry of twelve years from the date the cause of action accrued to him".[61]

Thus by the Limitation Act 1980 the law allows the right to land to be lost, the boundaries to land to be varied and a new title and boundary to be created.

Adverse possession requires first the discontinuance or dispossession of the paper title owner (PTO) followed by exclusive possession for the required period by the squatter coupled with a demonstrable intention to exclude everyone.

The first element therefore is the discontinuance or dispossession of the PTO. The squatter must show either that there has been an ouster of the PTO or a discontinuance of possession by the PTO. There is "a fairly heavy presumption that possession is retained by the paper title owner" which must be rebutted before time can begin to run in favour of the squatter.[62] The "slightest acts of ownership" on the part of PTO will rebut any suggestion that he has discontinued possession of his land.[63]

The second element necessary to successfully establish an adverse possession claim is the necessary degree of exclusive physical control for the required period, which will be considered later in this chapter.

---

61 Limitation Act 1980, section 15(1).
62 Gray *'Elements of Land Law'* 3rd. at p.259, *Williams Bros Direct Stores v Raftery* [1957] 3 All ER 593 and *Wallis's Clayton Bay Holiday Camp Ltd v Shell Mex* [1974] 3 All ER 575. But the rule applied in the last mentioned case, to the effect that time did not run in the squatter's favour where the PTO has some present *or future* use for his land, is no longer good law (para. 8(4), schedule 1, Limitation Act 1980).
63 *Buckingham County Council v Moran* [1990] 1 Ch. 623.

The third part of the definition is the *animus possidendi*, which is:

"The intention in one's own name and on one's own behalf to exclude the world at large".[64]

Finally, possession must be "adverse" to found a claim. As Slade J explained in *Buckinghamshire County Council v Moran*:[65]

"Possession is never adverse within the meaning of the 1980 Act if it is enjoyed under lawful title. If, therefore, a person occupies or uses land by licence of the owner and his licence has not been fully determined, he cannot be treated as having been in "adverse possession" as against the owner of the paper title."

However, the House of Lords have recently indicated that the squatter's willingness to pay for his occupation or use of the disputed land if asked is irrelevant to the establishment of a good claim and the term "adverse possession" has been criticised. It was not indicative of any absence of an intention to possess on the squatter's part and it was the intention to possess that was important not the intention to own. The words "possess" and "dispossess" were to be given their ordinary meaning so that implied consent did not matter. What would matter would be the actual consent of the PTO to the occupation of the squatter, which would be fatal to the possession of the disputed land being with the squatter.[66]

The doctrine of adverse possession is described in most of the leading textbooks[67] as being negative in its effect, i.e. it extinguishes the PTO's legal title but does not create a new legal title[68] for the squatter. In particular it extinguishes the PTO's remedy against the squatter for trespass, so that if the PTO is a tenant his landlord will still be able to enforce his covenants against the tenant and *vice versa*.

But, although all title is relative, a squatter's title is as good, indeed better, than a paper title since the squatter cannot be ousted by anyone once he establishes title by adverse possession.[69] Once the squatter's

---

64 Per Slade J in *Powell v Mc Farlane* (1977) 38 P & CR 452. This statement of the law has recently been approved by the House of Lords in *JA Pye (Oxford) Limited v Graham* [2002] 3 WLR 221, which adopted in large part Slade J's analysis in *Powell v Mc Farlane*.
65 [1990] 1 Ch. 623 at 636 H.
66 *JA Pye (Oxford) Limited v Graham* [2002] 3 WLR 221 at 233A–B (para. 37).
67 See, for example, Cheshire and Burn *'The Modern Law of Real Property'* 15th ed. (1994) p.847.
68 In the words of Baron Parke in *Doe'd Jukes v Sumner* (1845) 14 M and W 39 at 42, the strict effect of the passing of the 12-year period was "not to make a parliamentary conveyance".
69 *Fairweather v St Marylebone Property Co Ltd* [1963] AC 510.

claim is established the PTO's title to unregistered land is extinguished as is any claim to rent or mesne profits during the period of the squatter's occupation. The squatter's title once established is unchallengeable.[70]

In registered land the position is that once the limitation period has run its course the PTO is deemed to hold the land on trust for the squatter.[71] As well as being a beneficiary under that trust the squatter has an overriding interest in the land.[72] The register may be rectified in favour of the latter so that the squatter will be shown as paper title owner of the property.

Whilst many would question the role of adverse possession in a modern registration-based system[73] the rules are now well established and the courts have not, to date, found that they contravene the right to peaceful enjoyment of one's possessions under Article 1 of the First Protocol of the European Convention on Human Rights.[74] As we will see it has been left to Parliament to reform this unsatisfactory area of land law.[75] Until Land Registration Act 2002 comes into force[76] we must labour under its arcane rules as best we can. It is now necessary therefore to look at those rules in greater depth and in particular to consider the two key requirements of exclusive physical control and the necessary intention to possess.

---

70 *Cooke v Dunn* (1998) 9 BPR 16489.

71 Land Registration Act 1925, section 75(1), but under the Land Registration Act 2002 the device of the trust is no longer employed and the squatter, in the rare circumstance where he establishes title by adverse possession, may assert that proprietary right against the owner or against any third party purchaser.

72 Land Registration Act 1925, section 70(1)(f)–(g).

73 See *J A Pye (Oxford) Limited v Graham* [2000] 3 WLR 221 at 245 A (para. 73). As will be discussed later in this chapter, a substantial weakening of the present rights of the squatter will occur where the PTO's title is registered when the Land Registration Act 2002 becomes law. The squatter will be required to notify the Land Registry before title be extinguished and the Land Registry will notify the PTO. The PTO's objection would defeat the claim.

74 See *Family Housing Association v Donnellan* [2001] 30 EGCS 114 and *JA Pye (Oxford) Limited v Graham* CA [2001] Ch 804 approved by the House of Lords on this point at [2002] 3 WLR 221 at 244 H (para. 73) on the basis that the requirement in the Convention that UK legislation be interpreted compatibly with the Convention did not have retrospective effect.

75 The Law Commission proposed (in LC 270 and 271) that the primary limitation period should become 3 years starting from the date of knowledge (which was to have broadly the same definition as under section 14A of the Limitation Act 1980). There was to be a longstop of 10 years from the date of the accrual of the cause of action (i.e. the inception of possession by the squatter). The new law, as it was finally adopted by Parliament in the Land Registration Act 2002, is considered in greater detail at the end of this chapter.

76 The Land Registration Act 2002 is set to some into force on a date to be fixed by the Lord Chancellor.

5.2
Physical possession

Mere non-use by the PTO, even for a long period of time, will never found a squatter's claim to title by adverse possession.[77] The phrase "adverse possession" was directed not to the nature of the possession but to the capacity of the squatter. To establish factual possession the squatter had to show the absence of the PTO's consent together with a single and exclusive possession for the required period. In the majority of cases the squatter will have taken up physical possession in the sense that there will be no continuing acts of possession on the part of the PTO. Cases of ouster of the PTO are rare, but traditionally the courts have distinguished between cases of discontinuance and ouster.

The Court of Appeal in *Treloar* v *Nute*[78] described the difference between the "dispossession" (or ouster) and the assumption of possession by the squatter as follows:

> "The one is where a person comes in and drives out the other from possession, the other is where the person in possession goes out of possession and is followed by others."

But as Nourse LJ said in *Buckingham County Council* v *Moran*[79] the distinction between ouster and discontinuance is "a very fine one" and as the House of Lords have recently stressed[80] not the central question so far as the establishment of a valid adverse possession claim is concerned. As Lord Brown-Wilkinson said in *J A Pye (Oxford) Limited* v *Graham*:[81]

> "The question is simply whether the defendant squatter has dispossessed the paper title owner by going into ordinary possession of the land for the requisite period without the consent of the owner."

Buckinghamshire County Council v *Moran* was a case of discontinuance. In that case the claimant, the local authority, owned a plot of land which lay between two properties to its south and west but nothing separated it from the defendant's property to north. To the east

---

77 *Williams Bros Direct Supply Limited* v *Raftery* [1958] 1 QB 159.
78 [1976] 1 WLR 1295 at 1300.
79 *Supra.*
80 In *JA Pye (Oxford) Ltd* v *Graham* [2002] 3 WLR 221.
81 At 233 A (para.36).

lay a highway. The claimant had in mind that it might on a future date use the land for the purposes of diverting the highway. However, it took no steps to maintain it after about 1962. In 1967 the defendant's predecessor began to maintain the disputed land by trimming grass and maintaining hedges and in 1971 the disputed land was conveyed to the defendant for "all such rights and interests as the vendors had on or over" that land. Although the claimant became aware of the defendant's use of the disputed land in or about 1975 it did not bring ejectment proceedings until 1985.

It was held that in view of the fact that the defendant had assumed total physical control of the land by 1973, at the latest, by ensuring complete enclosure and annexation to his own house, it followed that the claimant's claim to possession failed. It mattered not that the claimant continued to have a future use of the land since it had not demonstrated that by taking any physical steps to maintain the land or assert its physical possession of the disputed land.

There is a presumption of continuing possession by the PTO. Intermittent or slight acts of possession only reinforce this presumption.[82] Particularly where larger pieces of land are involved, it will be assumed that the PTO remains in possession in the absence of strong evidence to the contrary. However where in a suburban housing estate two neighbours shared a common driveway but only one of those neighbours had paved the drive and parked his car there it was held that he had established the necessary degree of exclusive physical control for the purposes of ousting the title of the paper title owner to the driveway in question. This was so even though the eaves of the PTO's property projected over that driveway by some 18 inches.[83]

The importance of the *Moran*[84] decision is that it established that where the PTO retained the land for some future use, but had physically ceased to be in possession, the squatter might be able to establish title by adverse possession despite that future intended use. However, in such a situation "very clear evidence" of possessory acts and intentions is needed before a finding of adverse possession will be made. In *Moran* such an intention was manifest from the squatter's acts of placing a lock and chain on the gates to the disputed land, which were crucial pieces of evidence.

---

82 See *Morice v Evans* (1989), *Times* 27/2/89.
83 *Williams v Usherwood* (1983) 45 P & CR 235.
84 [1990] Ch 623.

In summary, possession must be "actual open continuous and exclusive" (and of course without the licence of the PTO).[85]

Where the squatter is in possession of part of a larger plot of land he will not be able to establish adverse possession of the whole unless it is necessary to give effect to wider contractual obligations in relation to the land as a whole.[86]

5.3
Animus possidendi

To establish title by adverse possession the law requires more than the necessary degree of physical control. The subjective intention to possess must also be established. However, the two questions are closely associated. Thus, for example, enclosure always represents strong evidence of the necessary *animus possidendi* but it is also strong evidence that the necessary degree of physical control has been established.

In the classic statement of the law by Slade J in *Powell v Mc Farlane:*[87]

"*Animus possidendi* requires the intention in one's own name and on one's own behalf, to exclude the world at large including the PTO...so far as is reasonably practical and so far the processes of law will allow".

What is required is the intention to *possess* not the intention to *own*.[88] In practice what will be required is evidence that the squatter "for the time being" intended to exclude others including the paper title owner".[89] However, it has been held that the required mental element does not extend to a requirement to exclude the PTO in all circumstances. The squatter must show however that he intended "to treat the land as though he were the occupying owner".[90] But in the *Pye* case, the House of Lords have made it plain that this intention was not necessarily contradicted by a willingness on the part of the squatter to pay for occupation of the land if asked to do so for that was consistent with an intention to possess.

---

85 *Shaw* v *Garbutt* (1996) 7 BPR 14816 at p.14827.
86 See *Glynn* v *Howell* [1909] 1 Ch. 666.
87 (1977) 38 P & CR 452 at 471, now approved by the House of Lords in *JA Pye (Oxford) Limited* v *Graham* (HL) [2002] 3 WLR 221.
88 *JA Pye (Oxford) Ltd* v *Graham* (HL) [2002] 3 WLR 221.
89 See *Buckingham County Council* v *Moran* [1990] Ch 623 at 644E.
90 *J A Pye (Oxford) Ltd* v *Graham* (HL) [2002] 3 WLR 221.

In the words of Slade J in *Powell* v *Mc Farlane*:

> "the squatter must bring forward clear and affirmative evidence not only that he intended to possess the land but to make that intention clear to the world."

The squatter must have behaved in a manner which objectively may be said to be consistent with his having exclusive possession of the land. Obviously the stronger the acts of possession relied on the more likely it is that the necessary intent may be inferred from those acts.

A number of acts of possession may be relevant both to the establishment of the necessary degree of physical control and the establishment of *animus possidendi*, for example, planting or felling trees, cutting grass, grazing cattle, fishing, turning away strangers and enclosing the land in question.

The House of Lords in the *Pye* case said that "possession" has its well-established meaning of having "sufficient control of the relevant land to entitle that person to bring an action for trespass".

5.4
The limitation periods in different classes of ownership

Time runs against the owner of the land for twelve years from the date that his cause of action accrues.[91] In the case of Crown, spiritual or eleemosynary land (by which is meant land belonging to the Church of England and not to other denominations) the period is 30 years.[92] Because the property of a company that has been dissolved vests in the Crown[93] as *bona vacantia* the 30-year rule will also apply in cases where the paper title vests in that company. The 30-year rule also applies in relation to dissolved companies that vest in the Royal Duchies. A company search in such a case should normally establish the present status of a company. However, in relation to certain corporations aggregate, such as the Church Commissioners for

---

91 Limitation Act 1980, section 15 and Schedule 1 paras 1 & 8.
92 Limitation Act 1980, Schedule 1 para 10.
93 Companies Act 1985, section 654.

England and the Oxbridge colleges, the 12-year rule applies. Foreshore owned by the Crown is subject to a 60-year limitation period.[94]

There is nothing to prevent time continuing to run in favour of a succession of squatters but time cannot continue to run where there is a break in possession, even if no other person is in possession for the period of that break.[95] If a second squatter (S2) dispossess the first (S1) he acquires the benefit of the time that has accrued in favour of the first but the first squatter retains the right to oust the second squatter for the full period of limitation from the time that he was dispossessed until that limitation period has run its course. Thus if S1 dispossesses PTO in 1976 and is then dispossessed by S2 in 1984, the PTO loses the right to bring possession proceedings in 1988 but S1 can regain possession against S2 until 1996 (i.e. 12 years after he was dispossessed). Time stops running if the squatter abandons the land at any time before the limitation period expires.

The above limitation periods are subject to other important exceptions in relation to persons suffering from a disability,[96] where fraud or deliberate concealment of a cause of action has occurred[97] or where there has been an operative mistake.[98]

Where the land held by the squatter is registered in the name of trustees the beneficiary's rights continue after the rights of trustees have been extinguished. Only qualified title will be registered therefore until the squatter is able to prove that the right of action of all beneficiaries have also been barred.[99] Also time does not run against one beneficiary whilst another remains in possession of the land.

Time ceases to run in the squatter's favour when the PTO commences an action against him for ejectment and not simply when the PTO asserts title.[1] Alternatively the squatter may provide a signed written acknowledgement of the paper title either himself or through his agent.[2] An oral offer to purchase the land the subject of the claim is treated as an acknowledgment of PTO's title.[3] An oral acknowledgement does not

---

94 Limitation Act 1980, schedule 1 para 11.
95 Limitation Act 1980, schedule 1, para 8(2).
96 Limitation Act 1980, section 38(2).
97 Limitation Act 1980, section 32.
98 Limitation Act 1980, section 28.
99 Limitation Act 1980, schedule 1, para 8(2).
1   *J A Pye (Oxford) Limited* v *Graham* [2002] 3 WLR 221.
2   Limitation Act 1980, section 29(2) and 30(1)–(2).
3   *Edginton* v *Clark* [1964] 1 QB 367.

have the same effect although it may have evidential significance.[4] An action for relief, which does not necessarily involve recovery of possession, will not amount to an assertion of title by the paper title owner. The issuing of proceedings, which are subsequently dismissed, does not constitute an assertion of the PTO's title.[5]

5.5
The Land Registration Act 2002

A guide to the new law

Under the Land Registration Act 2002[6] the law on adverse possession in relation to registered land will be radically reformed. Adverse possession will no longer extinguish a registered title but the squatter will be entitled to apply to be registered as proprietor after being in uninterrupted possession for ten years. The squatter will then acquire an indefeasible title if there is no opposition to his application but if the registered proprietor, any chargee or other person notified, opposes the application it will be rejected unless the squatter can bring himself within one of three conditions (see below). Following refusal, the PTO then has two years to commence possession proceedings. If he does not the squatter may again apply to be registered and will be registered whether or not the PTO objects. There are certain defences to an ejectment claim but those are consistent with the three conditions mentioned below.

Under the new Act title to land held by a chargee before redemption cannot be extinguished.[7]

The three conditions mentioned, where the squatter may acquire title by adverse possession despite an objection by the PTO, are:

1) Where the squatter can claim an equity by estoppel, for example proprietary estoppel.

---

4   See *J Pye (Oxford) Limited* v *Graham* (HL) [2002] 3 WLR 221.
5   *Markfield Investments Limited* v *Evans* [2001] 1 WLR 1321.
6   Which comes into force on a date to be fixed by the Lord Chancellor (section 136 (2)).
7   Land Registration Act 2002, section 96.

2) Where the squatter can establish "some other right to the land", for example where a purchaser of land paid the purchase price but was never registered as freehold proprietor.

3) Where the squatter made a reasonable mistake as to the boundary, for example where the boundary is fenced in ignorance of the plan lodged at the Land Registry showing the correct boundary position.

Rights acquired by a squatter or in the course of being acquired are overriding interests. However, under the new law, as under the old, a squatter may also protect himself by registering a caution so that any purchaser of the PTO's interest will be aware of his putative interest. At the time of writing the new Land Registration Rules have not yet been drafted but they are likely to contain similar provisions to the old in relation to the protection of squatter's rights.

The new Act will encourage registration by owners and is likely to reduce the number of claims by squatters.[8] The importance of the subject is also likely to reduce therefore and it is very much to be welcomed that injustice of the type seen in *J A Pye (Oxford) Limited* v *Graham* is likely to become much rarer. The new system will tie in better with a modern system of registered conveyancing and will no longer require examination of the ancient rules of possession.

---

8   Currently around 20,000 a year of which a surprising 15,000 are successful (Baroness Scotland of Asthall the Parliamentary Under Secretary of State at the Lord Chancellor's Department speaking during the passage of the Bill (Hansard (HL) 30th October 2001).

CHAPTER 6

Party structures and features

Party structures and features

6.1
The meaning of "party structure" and related expressions

A "party structure" is one that straddles the boundary between two parcels of land, which are in the ownership of different people, as opposed to a "boundary structure" which demarcates the boundary between two parcels of land at the furthest extent of one of those parcels. With certain refinements the same rules apply in relation to analysing a party hedge as a party wall, fence or other structure. The expression "party structure" is therefore generally to be preferred to "party wall". However, much of the legislation in the field uses the expression "party wall". Although the law is now largely contained in the Party Wall Act 1996, it helps to look at some earlier uses of the term "party wall" and related expressions before the modern definition is considered. It will also be necessary to consider the position at common law for those rare cases where the 1996 Act does not provide the answer.

The London Building (Amendment) Act 1939, which formerly applied to land within the London Boroughs, defined a "party wall" as:

> "A wall which forms part of a building and stands on lands of different owners to a greater extent than the projection of any artificially formed support on which the wall rests."[9]

The 1939 Act had a separate definition of "party fence wall"[10] as:

> "A wall (not being part of a building) which stands on lands of different owners and is used or constructed to be used for separating such adjoining lands, but does not include a wall constructed on the land of one owner the artificially formed support of which projects into the land of another."

---

9   London Building (Amendment) Act 1939, section 44; considered in greater detail below.
10 London Building (Amendment) Act 1939, section 4.

The Party Wall Act 1996 ("the 1996 Act") also defines a "party fence wall" as a structure which stands on the land of more than one person but which is not part of a building.[11]

It is possible to find a structure that constitutes a party structure along some of its length and a boundary structure along another part.[12]

The law on party walls is now essentially contained in the 1996 Act, by which Parliament applied nationally,[13] with modifications, rules which previously applied locally to the London Boroughs under the London Building Act 1939 and to an assortment of other areas, for example, in Bristol. The 1996 Act will be considered after the rules that applied at common law are summarised, because the common law rules continue to be important in a variety of situations.

6.2
Rights between neighbours owning party structures at common law

A boundary structure may become a party structure because that is the way it is defined in the deeds or because that is an inference that can be drawn from the surrounding circumstances. Thus, in *Burns* v *Morton*[14] the Court of Appeal had to consider whether the reference to a "dividing structure" in a conveyance amounted to an expression of an intention by the parties to that conveyance that the wall concerned was to demarcate the boundary between the two properties. It was held that it did and thus the wall in question constituted a party wall.

Walls which divide properties, e.g. in a terrace, are normally party walls in the absence of express provision to the contrary.

The conveyance or transfer from which the title to the land in question is derived normally covers the demarcation of party and boundary structures and the rights of repair and support. In the absence of express provision of this type, where, as a matter of construction, the structure dividing two properties is a party structure, mutual easements

---

11 Party Wall Act 1996, section 20. The definitions in the 1996 Act are considered in greater detail later in this chapter.

12 *Dean* v *Walker* (1997) 73 P & CR 366.

13 See Hansard HL Debates vol. 568 31/1/96.

14 [2000] 1 WLR 347.

of support automatically arise as between the two owners so that neither owner may remove the right of support that the other enjoys.

There is thought to be a natural right of support to land from the land of a neighbour provided that the support has been derived as long as the land has been in existence.[15] But, it is generally thought that the natural right of support of land for land does not extend to a building or structure placed on neighbouring land, which constitutes an additional burden on that land.[16] In many cases it might be relevant to establish that the actions of the neighbour in carrying out excavations to his land constitute a threat to a building or structure on neighbouring land. To protect such a building or structure, in the absence of express provision in the deeds, it is necessary to establish that an easement of support has been acquired,[17] for example, by prescription or under the rule in *Wheeldon* v *Burrows*.[18]

In the case of prescription, it is necessary to establish 20 years continuous user as of right, provided the owner of the servient land has not for any part of that 20 year period been under a disability (for example because he was a child). Where the servient owner was under such a disability 40 years is the correct period. In order to establish the right by the owner of land not to have the removal of the lateral support his land naturally derives from his neighbour's land (as opposed to his buildings), it would be necessary to prove that the building had derived support from the neighbour's land for a period of twenty years (i.e. the period required for acquisition by prescription) and that land had been removed before an action could be successfully brought.

In the absence of an easement of support the owner of land adjoining land on which his neighbour has constructed a building is under no obligation to ensure that his neighbour's property does not fall down, for example, through settlement on his land. It is not thought that he is under a positive duty to shore up his neighbour's property before he carries out excavation works save in so far as he would have been under such an obligation if there were no building or structure on the adjoining land.[19]

---

15 See *Gale on Easements* 17th ed. at 10–02.

16 *Dalton* v *Angus* (1881) 6 App. Cas. 740.

17 *Gale on Easements* 17th ed at 10–16 et seq.

18 (1879) 12 Ch. D. 31, but clearly an easement of support under *Wheeldon* v *Burrows* cannot be acquired where a building said to be entitled to that support was not on the quasi-dominant tenement at the date of the transfer out of one ownership (see *Kebewar Pty Ltd* v *Harkin* (1987) 9 NSWLR 738).

19 See *Dalton* v *Angus, supra*.

But, the law of nuisance and negligence was often relevant in this area to fill in gaps that were not adequately filled by the law of easements. In the absence of any natural right of support (which was for land as opposed to buildings) or an easement of support, it was frequently necessary to prove negligence, nuisance or a right of action under the rule in *Rylands* v *Fletcher*.[20]

It has been held,[21] for example, that there may be a positive obligation on a landowner to prevent or reduce the risk of foreseeable injury or damage to a neighbour. But, at common law, the rights of neighbours are largely negative in character, for example, either party has the right to enter the land of his neighbour for the purposes of abating a nuisance.

Problems often used to arise where the property did not fall within one of the areas governed by the various local statutory codes for party walls that applied before the commencement of the 1996 Act and where there was no express provision in the deeds governing the ownership of or support for a structure at or adjoining the boundary. Illustrative of the problems that used to arise is the case of *Bradburn* v *Lindsay*.[22]

In that case two semi-detached properties were divided from each other by a party wall. The owner of one of those properties allowed the party wall to fall into disrepair and eventually that property was demolished by the local authority. Once the remains of the party wall were exposed to the elements further damage ensued and the owner of the extant property brought proceedings against the owner of the adjoining land claiming that the right of support, which he had hitherto enjoyed, had been removed. He also brought a claim in nuisance and negligence.

Blackett-Ord V–C held that since L should reasonably have appreciated the danger from dry rot and lack of repair and there were steps he could reasonably have taken to prevent the damage, he owed a duty to B to take these steps and by failing to do so was liable for the damage caused. B was entitled to support in the form of buttresses that supported his building.

However, as has been mentioned above, a right of support is generally thought to be negative character, i.e. it does not give rise to a positive obligation to maintain the party structure, it merely gives rise

---

20 (1866) LR 1Exch 265.

21 In *Leakey* v *National Trust* [1980] QB 485.

22 [1983] 2 All ER 408.

to cross easements of support whereby neither party may deprive the other of that right. In particular using a wall of a neighbour for support does not give title by adverse possession but merely to easements of support.[23] But by making extensive provision for maintenance, support and dispute resolution the 1996 Act has lessened the need to rely on these common law rights.

6.3
The statutory scheme for the resolution of disputes involving party structures under the Party Wall Act 1996

As we have seen the Party Wall Act 1996[24] applied nationally principles for the determination of ownership and maintenance of party structures which previously applied locally, within London under the London Building Act 1939 and in certain other areas under various pieces of local legislation. Those miscellaneous pieces of legislation have now been repealed leaving only the 1996 Act in place. The Act, which came into force on 1st July 1997, creates a scheme of notices and counter notices whereby wherever possible the parties agree that a structure is or is not a party structure prior to construction. The Act further makes provision for certain work to existing party structures to be at the parties' joint expense and also contains provisions in relation to boundary structures and thus is of greater importance than its title would seem to suggest.

The following definitions are used in the 1996 Act:[25]

'"Party fence wall" means a wall (not being part of a building) which stands on lands of different owners and is used or constructed to be used for separating such adjoining lands, but does not include a wall constructed on the land of one owner the artificially formed support of which projects into the land of another owner';

---

23 *Phillipson* v *Gibbon* (1871) 6 Ch App 428.
24 For a helpful introduction see the DETR explanatory booklet 'The Party Wall etc Act 1996' (code 99CD 0018) and Bickford-Smith and Sydenham 'Party Walls – the New Law' (1997) Jordans.
25 In section 20.

'"Party structure" means a wall and also a floor partition or other structure separating buildings or parts of buildings approached solely by separate staircases or separate entrances';

'"Party wall" means–

"(a) A wall which forms part of a building and stands on lands of different owners to a greater extent than any artificially formed support on which the wall rests; and

(b) So much of the wall not being a wall referred to in paragraph (a) above as separates buildings belonging to different owners."

Section 1 of the 1996 Act makes provision for new building on the line of the junction between two adjoining owners' land. Before any owner may build on the line of the junction between his and his neighbour's land he shall at least one month before he carries out such work serve a notice which indicates his desire to do so and the nature of the intended wall.[26] If the owner on whom the notice is served indicates by notice that he consents to the proposed wall it shall be built half on the land of each owner or in such other position as shall be agreed and the expense thereof shall be shared according to the use to be made by them of the wall and the cost of labour and materials then prevailing. If the adjoining owner does not consent to the wall being on the boundary line the wall may only be built on the owners' land at his expense.

Where the owner building the wall wishes to build it wholly on his own land he must nevertheless give his neighbour notice one month before construction begins. Where he complies with the notice requirement he shall, notwithstanding any objections, be entitled to place the footings of the wall on his neighbours land provided construction does not take place more than 12 months after the notice.[27] Where the owner served with the notice does not consent the owner serving the notice must build the wall at his own expense and shall compensate the other owner for any damage arising.[28]

---

26 Section 1(2).
27 Section 1(6).
28 Section 1(7).

Section 2 (1) provides for repair and maintenance of existing party walls. The section applies where–

"Lands of different owners adjoin and at the line of junction the said lands are built on or a boundary wall, being a party fence wall or the external wall of a building, has been erected".

Section 2 (2) gives the building owner wide rights over the land of his neighbour, for example, to "underpin, thicken or raise a party structure or party fence wall", to "make good, repair or demolish and rebuild a party structure or party fence wall in a case where such work is necessary on account of defect or want of repair of the structure or wall", to demolish a party structure which is of insufficient strength or height for any intended building, to cut into a party structure for the purpose of fitting a damp proof course, to cut away from a party wall, party fence wall, external wall or boundary wall any footing or projecting chimney breast or other projection in order to enable a vertical wall to be erected or raised against the wall or building of the adjoining owner and to "execute any other necessary works incidental to the connection of a party structure with premises adjoining it".

Save in the case of want of repair the above works are exercisable subject to making good all damage occasioned by the work to the adjoining premises, their furnishings or decorations and, where appropriate, carrying all flues or chimney stacks up to such height and in such materials as may be agreed with the building owner. There are other detailed provisions contained within section 2 which must be studied before certain specific types of work are carried out.

It should be noted that section 2 does not apply to building works commenced before 1st September 1997. Secondly, the right in section 2 (2)(b) to demolish a party fence wall does not appear to give the owner the right to rebuild it to a lesser height than previously.

Before carrying out any of the work contained in section 2 a "party structure notice" must be served in accordance with section 3. Such a notice should contain the name and address of the building owner, the nature of and particulars of the proposed work including, where the construction of foundations is involved, detailed particulars of the loads to be carried etc and the date that the proposed work is to begin. Such notice shall be served two months before the work is to begin and shall cease to have effect if the work is not commenced within two months and prosecuted with due diligence.

Service of the structure notice is thought, as with service of a notice under section 47 of the 1939 Act, to supersede the common law right to support from the wall.[29]

The owner served with a notice may then serve a counter notice under section 4 which requires the owner carrying out the work to "build in or on the wall such chimney copings, breasts, jambs or flues, or such piers or recesses or other like works, as may be reasonably be required for the convenience of the adjoining owner". Where work to the foundations is involved the owner served with the notice may request that the foundations shall go to a greater depth than that proposed and be of sufficient strength to bear the load of any intended building of the adjoining owner. The counter notice shall specify the works required and be served within a period of one month of the notice on him. The owner served with the counter notice shall comply with the counter notice unless he can show, for example, that it would cause him unnecessary inconvenience.[30]

Unless the notice or counter notice is responded to within the time period allowed (14 days) the recipient shall be deemed to have dissented from it and a dispute shall be deemed to have arisen between the parties.[31]

Where the building owner wishes to erect a building within three metres of the building or structure of an adjoining owner – and the foundations of that building will within the three metres extend below the level of the foundations of the adjoining owner – the building owner may, and where required by the adjoining owner, shall, strengthen or safeguard the foundations of that adjoining owner's building or structure in so far as it is necessary to do so.[32]

Where it is proposed to build within six metres (measured horizontally from any building or structure of an adjoining owner) and within those six metres that building or structure shall meet a plane drawn downwards in the direction of the excavation, building or structure the building owner may, and if required by the adjoining owner shall underpin, or otherwise strengthen the building or structure of the adjoining owner.[33]

---

29 See *Selby v Whitbread and Co* [1917] 1 KB 736.
30 Section 4(3).
31 Section 5.
32 Section 6(3).
33 Section 6.

There are notice requirements under section 6 as under other sections of the Act. The owner proposing to carry out the work shall not less than one month before commencing work serve a notice stating his proposals and indicate whether he proposes to underpin or otherwise. As well as making detailed provision as to the content of notices under section 6 that section provides[34] that if the adjoining owner does not indicate his consent to the work he shall be deemed to have dissented from the notice and a dispute shall be deemed to have arisen. In common with many of the other notice requirements of the Act a failure to begin the work within 12 months of the notice and prosecute the work with due diligence shall cause the notice to cease to have effect. Section 6 does not apply to works, which commenced before 1st September 1997.

Section 7 deals with compensation. A building owner shall compensate his neighbour for any loss and damage arising out of any work under the Act.

Section 8 gives the owner executing the work certain rights over his neighbour's land. Generally such entry must be on notice (given 14 days before such work begins) but in an emergency may be such notice as is "reasonably practicable".

The Act is stated not to affect any easement relating to a party wall or any right to light or a right to support arising from that right[35] but as I have mentioned in relation to party structure notices[36] a notice under section 3 of the Act is thought to supersede any common law right to support for the structure in question.

Dispute resolution is dealt with either by appointing a single surveyor or by each neighbour appointing his own surveyor followed by a third appointed by those surveyors.[37] The single surveyor or any two of the three surveyors determine the dispute. An appeal lies to the county court.

In deciding the principles upon which the award should be made the surveyor or surveyors is not able to compensate for loss of trade but must stick to those matters set out in section 10.[38]

Where expense is incurred in repairing a party structure or party fence wall and the work is necessary because of a defect in or want of

---

34 In section 6(7).
35 In sections 6(10) and 9.
36 At p. 72 footnote 226.
37 Section 10.
38 See the cases decided under the equivalent provision in the 1939 Act (section 55).

repair the expenses thereof shall be defrayed in the proportions which have regard to the use they make of that structure or wall and to the cause of that defect in or want of repair.[39] Compensation shall be paid to the adjoining owner for disturbance and inconvenience caused by demolition work to the party structure where "the adjoining premises are laid open" in exercise of this right.

Section 12 contains provision for security for expenses and section 13 makes provision for accounts within two months of completing work for which expenses are to be wholly or partly to be defrayed by the adjoining owner. Section 14 to 19 contain, for example, provisions dealing with the service of notices and the application of the Act to certain land (Crown land is covered by the Act).

The Act is to be welcomed in assimilating practice nationwide. Of note are the tight time limits imposed. However, the terminology in the Act is different in places from that commonly used by conveyancers, e.g. in determining where the liability for the expense involved in constructing a party wall or party fence wall the Act refers to the cost being shared having regard to "the use made or to be made of the wall by each of them and to the cost of labour and materials prevailing at the time that the use is made by each owner respectively".[40] This is in contrast to the frequently used expression in conveyances and transfers to the effect that party walls are to be repairable at their "joint expense" or "shared equally".[41] Preliminary inquiries before contract should therefore continue to seek details of any awards there have been prior to a sale.

No reported cases appear to have been decided under the new Act at the time of writing, which appears to indicate that the Act works relatively well in practice.

---

39 Section 11(5).
40 Section 1(3)(b).
41 It was the view of the Conveyancer ((1996) 60 Conv September/October 326) when the Act was passed that in such circumstances it is quite possible that contribution obligations could be enforced as before.

6.4
Access to neighbouring land

The Access to Neighbouring Land Act 1992[42] was introduced to plug a loophole in the law. Prior to its introduction, in the absence of express provision being made in the deeds of the property, it was necessary to show an implied easement to maintain or repair a building before access to a neighbour's land could be gained. Whilst most neighbours were prepared to accede to their neighbour's requests for access problems did occur from time to time. However, whilst the Act may be useful in certain circumstances its provisions have largely been superseded by the Party Wall Act 1996 and it is therefore dealt with here.

The Act gives a statutory right of access for the purposes of carrying out work to one's land. This is facilitated by means of an access order by which the dominant owner may enter the land of the servient owner in order to carry out works to his land. Before it will grant an access order, however, the court[43] must be satisfied that the works are reasonably necessary for the preservation of the whole or any part of the dominant land and they cannot be carried out, or would be substantially more difficult to carry out, without entry upon the servient land.[44] But the court shall not make an access order:

> "in any case where it is satisfied that, were it to make such an order—
>
> (a) the respondent or any other person would suffer interference with, or disturbance of, his use or enjoyment of the servient land or,
>
> (b) the respondent, or any other person...in occupation of the whole or any part of the servient land, would suffer hardship
>
> to such degree by reason of the entry... that it would be unreasonable to make the order".[45]

---

42 Which came into force on 31 January 1993.
43 By virtue of article 6A of the High Court and County Court Jurisdiction Order 1991 (IS 1991/724) all applications under this Act must be commenced in the county court but both the county court and the High Court have jurisdiction to try cases.
44 Section 1(2).
45 Section 1(3).

6.5
Trees and fences

Trees and fences are frequently used as party as well as boundary features and thus warrant separate attention here.

Trees

A tree on the boundary will *prima facie* belong to the person who planted it.[46] Where the tree is ancient and it cannot therefore be ascertained who planted it, acts of pruning or lopping may provide evidence of ownership.[47] There may be cases, however, where the tree has been planted right up to the boundary and the roots and branches may grow unto the adjoining land. In that situation it is possible that the tree will become jointly owned.[48] However it is much more likely that such a tree would be regarded as solely owned by the owners of the land on whose land it was planted, if that can be established.[49]

The right of the adjoining owner to lop branches overhanging his land will be considered elsewhere.[50] Where the neighbour affected does not take pre-emptive action in this way he may have a claim for a *quia timet* injunction to protect the value of his land and/or a claim for damages.

Damage is frequently caused by tree roots, which apply pressure to the sub-soil and sometimes cause collapse settlement to buildings and structures above.[51] Where this occurs the neighbour whose land is affected in that way may bring an action in nuisance against the neighbour responsible for the damage. In an appropriate case an injunction may be granted to compel the neighbour who owns a tree, which threatens the structural integrity of a property, to remove the tree in question.[52] In many cases actions have successfully been brought against local authorities responsible for damage caused by tree roots on

---

46 *Masters* v *Pollie* (1620) 2 Roll Rep 141.
47 *Davey* v *Harrow Corporation* [1958] 1 QB 60 at 70.
48 As in *Waterman* v *Soper* (1698) 1 Ld Raym 737.
49 *Elliot* v *London Borough of Islington* [1991] 1 EGLR 167.
50 See section 9.1 of chapter 9.
51 See *Mc Combe* v *Read* [1955] 2 QB 429.
52 However for any action in nuisance to succeed it must first be established that the person sued has sufficient interest in the land in question (see *Hunter* v *Canary Wharf Limited* [1997] 2 WLR 684).

highways. Such damage frequently involves the cost of underpinning a property adjoining that highway.[53]

The right to overhang with branches or to grow roots under a neighbours land cannot normally give rise to prescriptive rights in the nature of easements or to adverse possession claims, in view of the gradual encroachment that by nature occurs.[54] But obviously the question of whether the neighbour affected by an overhanging tree has an easement of the light is a highly relevant factor. Where such an easement is established he may claim the removal of any branches that interfere with that right.

Where a tree, shrub or hedge overhangs a neighbour's land, but is in danger of falling over, a court is likely to make an access order under the Access to Neighbouring Land Act 1992 since any refusal of access is likely to be considered unreasonable.

Fences

Fences frequently constitute party or boundary features and are therefore subject to the rules which apply to the determination of disputes relating to such features, for example, under the Party Wall Act 1996. However, there are certain characteristics of fences that warrant separate consideration.

A "fence" has been defined as:

> "Any kind of enclosure or division but a hedge ditch or wall will most commonly be found to answer that description".[55]

Thus the definition in a deed of "fence" is frequently intended to cover any erection that prevents the invasion of animals or people onto the land in question. On the other hand a fence has been held not to be a "building or erection" for the purposes of a local Act which prohibited the making of a building or erection within ten feet of a wharf.[56]

In the absence of an enforceable agreement to do so or an easement which has been acquired by one of the recognised methods, for example, prescription or implied grant, there is no general duty on a

---

53 As occurred in *Delaware Mansions Limited* v *Westminster City Council* [2002] 1 AC 321, HL.
54 See *Lemon* v *Webb* [1895] AC 1.
55 Woolrych *'The Law on Party Walls and Fences'* p.281.
56 *AG and Great Yarmouth Port Authority* v *Harrison* (1920) 89 LJ Ch 607, CA.

landowner to fence his land.[57] However there is a duty under the Animals Act 1971 to prevent animals straying on to an adjoining highway or onto a neighbour's land. Under that Act "fencing" includes any obstacle erected to prevent the escape of animals.[58]

Where the duty to fence exists it is normally a duty to maintain a fence between adjoining properties but it does not carry with it a right to enter the neighbouring property unless that right is expressly granted.[59] But an implied right may be said to exist where the only method of fulfilling the duty is to enter the neighbours land and clearly the power contained in the Access to Neighbouring Land Act 1992 to grant an access order is likely to be relevant here also.[60]

The duties to fence that arise for the owner of land adjoining a highway are complex. No such duty existed at common law save where there is an artificial structure or object on land that would create a public nuisance if it were not fenced.[61] But there is an important duty to fence land that adjoins a highway under section 165 of the Highways Act 1980 where there is anything on the land that is a source of danger to those using that highway. There are also numerous other statutory duties to fence that are beyond the scope of this book.[62]

---

57 *Star* v *Rookesby* (1710) 1 Salk 335.
58 See sections 8 and 11.
59 See *Sutcliffe* v *Holmes* [1947] KB 147 at 154.
60 See Aldridge '*Boundaries Walls and Fences*' at chapter 5.
61 See *Barnes* v *Ward* (1850) 9 CB 392 and *Hounsell* v *Smyth* (1860) 7 CB (NS) 731.
62 The reader is referred to *Halsbury's Laws* Fourth Edition 2002 re-issue volume 4(1) at paragraph 948 for a fuller discussion.

CHAPTER 7

Establishing the boundary in particular cases

Establishing the boundary in particular cases

7.1
Highways and ownership of their sub-soil

A highway may be created by express statutory dedication or at common law by dedication and acceptance.[63] Dedication and acceptance may be inferred from a long period of user by members of the public. Acceptance imparts an obligation on the part of the local authority to maintain the highway in question.[64]

There is a presumption that where land is conveyed or transferred adjoining a highway or private right of way the conveyance or transfer operates to transfer ownership up to the middle of that highway[65] or private right of way.[66] The presumption (in Latin the *ad medium filum viae* presumption) is that, in the absence of evidence to the contrary,[67] a conveyance or transfer of land adjoining the highway operates to transfer the sub-soil of the highway up to the centre line of the highway and the airspace above, subject only to the right of passage of those entitled to use the surface.

The presumption will apply even though the conveyance or transfer refers to the land conveyed or transferred as being bounded by the highway in question.

The presumption will apply in the case of a development of a building estate despite the absence of a reference to the property conveyed or transferred including any part of the adjoining road, indeed the parcels may in some cases contradict such a presumption.[68] The conveyance of the sub-soil to the middle of an adjoining highway

---

63 *DPP* v *Jones* [1999] 2 AC 240.
64 See Stephen Sauvain '*Highway Law*' 2nd ed..
65 *Berridge* v *Ward* (1861) 10 CB (NS) 400.
66 *Smith* v *Howden* (1863) 14 CB (NS) 398.
67 *London and North Western Rly* v *Mayor of Westminster* [1902] 1 Ch 269.
68 *Giles* v *County Building Constructors* (1971) 22 P & CR 978.

may have important implications for the house owner concerned because with ownership of part of a highway is likely to come the obligation to pay for the adoption of the highway. But the presumption may be rebutted by appropriate evidence to the contrary, for example, the presumption of the ownership of the sub-soil vesting in the adjoining owner is rebutted by evidence that the adjoining owner was not intended to take any part of the highway.[69]

But whilst the 50% ownership rule may have disadvantages for the adjoining owner it may also have advantages. The ownership by the highway authority of the surface does not extend to the subsoil other than the immediate subsoil so that the adjoining owner has the right to the minerals beneath the highway.

In registered land it is a feature of the general boundaries rule, reflected in Land Registry practice, that no part of the highway is shown as being part of an adjoining owner's registered title even where the presumption of 50% ownership applies.[70]

It has been recognised that where the highway authority actually has the surface vested in it (e.g. following dedication) the highway authority has legal estate to the surface of the land and such part of the sub-soil as is necessary for the performance of its statutory functions.[71]

The adjoining owner by virtue of the fact that the roots of a tree growing on his property extend beneath the surface of the highway can cause damage to the surface of the highway. Because he is the owner of the sub-soil of the highway he may be the owner of the tree and thus liable in public nuisance to a user of the highway who is affected by that tree[72] but in practice the highway authority has the right and is under a statutory duty to remove a tree which constitutes a nuisance.[73] Indeed the highway authority is under a duty to maintain trees which are planted in a highway, whether they were planted before or after the highway was dedicated.[74]

The day-to-day problems with the management of such trees and the frequent problems with liability that may arise therefore remain with the highway authority. Where the highway is adopted the local authority has

---

69 See for e.g. *Mappin Bros.* v *Liberty and Co Ltd* [1903] 1 Ch 118.
70 See *Russell* v *London Borough of Barnet* [1984] 2 EGLR 44.
71 *Tithe Redemption Commission* v *Runcorn UDC* [1954] Ch. 383.
72 See *Clerk and Lindsell on Torts* 18th ed.19–106 et seq..
73 See *Stillwell* v *New Windsor Corporation* [1932] 2 Ch 155.
74 Highways Act 1980, section 96.

the duty to repair and maintain the surface of the highway and is normally liable for injury, loss and damage to third parties.[75]

A stopping up order in relation to a highway will only extinguish public rights over the surface of the highway and will not necessarily affect ownership. Where an order stopping up a highway is made the surface of the highway reverts to the legal owner for the duration of that stopping up order. Obviously, the position will be otherwise where the surface of the highway has been sold, rather than dedicated, to the highway authority.

Where a highway is fenced it will be assumed that the highway extends up to that fence provided it can be shown that the fence was erected to divide a close or closes from the highway. Land adjoins a highway for this purpose even where it is physically separated from it by a footpath, which is itself a public right of way.[76] The presumption will not apply when the fence pre-dated the highway. The same principles will apply to hedges adjoining highways.

7.2
Rainwater goods, spouts and projections

As we have seen[77] a conveyance, lease or transfer of property passes the airspace above it and the land beneath it.[78]

However, on the conveyance or transfer of a property, be it leasehold or freehold, there is a presumption that the entirety passes, including any projecting eaves, rainwater goods or footings but not the airspace between any foundations, which project over the boundary line, and any projections that overhang that boundary line.[79] But, where a plan is referred to (which is not contradicted by the parcels clause) and that plan shows, by reference to a particular floor plan, that the area shown includes part of any neighbouring building which overhangs the property conveyed[80] that will normally be decisive.

---

75 Highways Act 1980, section 41.

76 *Ware Urban District Council* v *Gaunt* [1960] 1 WLR 1364.

77 In chapter 3, where this subject is dealt with further.

78 It has been held that this principle applied where there was a conveyance of a property with a cellar beneath even though access to that cellar could only be gained via an adjoining retained property (*Grigsby* v *Melville* [1973] 3 All ER 455).

79 *Truckell* v *Stock* [1957] 1 WLR 161.

80 *Laybourn* v *Gridley* [1892] 2 Ch 53.

7·3
Boundaries of properties adjoining water courses, rivers, lakes and the seashore

A similar rule as applies in relation to land conveyed adjoining a highway applies in the case of land conveyed adjoining a non-tidal river or waterway. An *ad medium* presumption applies in relation to land up to the centre line of that river or waterway. However the physical process of aluvion (an addition to title) and diluvion (a subtraction from title) are also relevant.

Ownership to the midline of any watercourse does not carry with it the ownership of any island in the middle of the watercourse. The riparian owner's boundary extends by presumption up to the midline of the watercourse between the bank and the island.[81] The ends of the island facing upstream and downstream appear not to have been the subject of any litigation and therefore must be resolved by the normal principles of contract and conveyance as must ownership of the island itself.

In tidal rivers the exposure of any area of land previously covered by water will have the effect of vesting that additional piece or those additional pieces of land in the relevant riparian owner. Where, however, tidal rivers are involved land exposed at the bed of the river vets in the Crown. The rights of the Crown end with the point where the river ceases to ebb and flow.[82]

Where a fishery adjoins a river there is a presumption that the owner of that fishery also owns the freehold of the bed of the river.[83]

The doctrine of accretion applies to all land that has a water boundary. Ownership of such land changes according to the accretion or diluvion which applies whatever the boundary shown on the plan to the conveyance or transfer and whatever the description in the parcels clause. Thus over time the riparian owner may see his boundary advance or subtract.[84] The land added includes land which, under the rule relating to the beds of tidal rivers, formerly vested in the Crown.[85] Land added by accretion is subject to the same leasehold or other

---

81 See *Great Torrington Commons Conservators* v *Moore Stevens* [1904] 1 Ch 347.
82 *Ingram* v *Percival* [1969] 1 QB 548.
83 *Holford* v *Bailey* (1849) 13 QB 426 at 444.
84 *Lopez* v *Muddun Mohun Thakoor* (1870) 13 Moo Ind App 467.
85 *Re Hull and Selby Rly Co* (1839) 5 M & W 327.

interests as the land to which the accretion took place. Accretion or diluvion may be expressly excluded, but only by clear words.[86]

The doctrine of accretion does not apply to rivers which entirely change their course as opposed to gradually imperceptibly changing over a period of time as usually occurs and this applies whether the river is tidal or non tidal.

Unlike the ocean bed and the bed of tidal rivers, which vest in the Crown, the bed of a lake vests in the owner of the land and the ordinary rules for determining title apply. A lake wholly within one title will automatically pass without reference being made to it. Where the lake is in the ownership of the neighbour, unless the conveyance or transfer provides expressly to the contrary, the boundary will be the normal edge of the lake.[87] Where the lake is bounded by several different properties it is possible for one owner to have sole ownership whether by reference to his title deeds or by virtue of long user.[88] The rules as to accretion that apply to rivers do not apply to lakes.

The boundary line between the seashore and the adjoining land is, in the absence of evidence to the contrary, the median line of the high tide between the spring and neap tides.[89] With the seashore as with tidal rivers the tides change and the line of the tides change from time to time so that any conveyance or transfer by which title to the seashore is conveyed or transferred will necessarily be a moveable freehold.[90] A fixed freehold may only result where the clear words or phrases are used.[91]

The reference in a conveyance to a "beach" may have the same meaning as a reference to "the seashore"[92] but it can include land apparently adjoining the seashore at high tide, for example up to a physical barrier or road.

Section 61 of the Land Registration Act 2002[93] will provide that where the registered owner of land is shown as having a particular boundary (whether general or fixed) it will not affect the operation of accretion or diluvion. Whilst it will be perfectly possible for the parties, who are, for example, separated by a river, to agree that the boundaries

---

86 As in *Baxendale* v *Instow Parish Council* [1982] Ch 14.
87 See *Southern Centre for Theosophy* v *State of South Australia* [1982] AC 706 especially at p.716.
88 *Mackenzie and Bankes* (1878) 3 App Cas 1324.
89 See *AG* v *Chambers* (1854) 4 De GM & G 206.
90 *Scratton* v *Brown* (1825) 4 B and C 485.
91 *Baxendale* v *Instow Parish Council* [1982] Ch 14.
92 See *Government of the State of Penang* v *Beng Hong Oon* [1972] AC 425.
93 At the date of writing a date for the commencement of the Act has not been set.

between their respective properties should not change, that agreement would need to be recorded for it to be enforceable.[94]

---

94 LRA 2002, section 61(1).

Establishing ownership of the sub-soil

Establishing ownership of the sub-soil

8.1
Mines and quarries

Prima facie ownership of land extends to the centre of the earth beneath it and up to the heavens above it.[95] But, in relation to the sub-soil, there may be a number of reservations out of the land conveyed in respect of valuable mineral rights.

Where such reservations exist the person with the benefit of valuable minerals will have the right to carry away and profit from those minerals. This will include the right to construct mineshafts and construct roads for carrying away those minerals. However it does not include the right to destroy the surface of the land. Indeed there will be an obligation on the owner of the mineral rights to support the land above because the owner of surface of the land is entitled to the support he derives from the land below.

It will be appreciated that the ordinary rules by which easements and profits a prendre may be acquired may be important when considering mines and minerals. Many of the principles discussed above in relation to the ascertainment of the boundary position are also important to mines and minerals but as we shall see certain special problems arise.

However, the freehold owner's rights over minerals beneath his land are limited by certain common-law rules and there are a number of statutory provisions which are important. In particular all unworked coal reserves are vested by statute in the Coal Authority[96] and rights to oil and gas are vested in the Crown by statute.[97] Gold and silver is vested in the Crown at common law.

---

95 But the airspace above is typically not regarded as extending beyond about 200 yards above the roof level of any building constructed there. See also chapter 3.
96 Coal Industry Act 1994, sections 1(1) and 7(3).
97 Petroleum Act 1998, section 1.

8.2
Conveyancing problems associated
with ownership of mineral rights

A conveyance of land with a reservation out of the "mines and minerals" beneath will exclude every substance that can be removed from under the land for the purposes of profit.[98] Although there is often no express definition of the minerals that form part of the sub-soil, as opposed to those which form part of the surface of the land, the person who is granted or to whom is reserved the right to work minerals can, in practice, extract any mineral below the surface of the land. But it is necessary to check certain legislation to ensure that the mineral in question is not excluded from such a conveyance.[99]

A grant or reservation of mineral rights operates as a conveyance and the rules of construction discussed above[1] therefore apply. Where there is a reservation of mining rights to the surface of the land that is a matter which can often be determined relatively easily because it will be similar in its effect to any other reservation over land on a conveyance. However considerable problems arise in relation to mining leases of a particular seam or vein beneath the surface of the land. Determining the boundary between one seam and another may be a matter of complexity. A court considering a boundary dispute of this nature will look at the intentions of the parties in order to come to a common sense conclusion.[2]

Lord Denning defined the term "mines and minerals" in the parcels of a conveyance or *habendum* of a lease as including:

> "Every substance which can be got from underneath the surface of the earth for the purpose of profit".[3]

Thus the definition would include sand and gravel extraction and gas, which in the case of old conveyances had no economic value. But that definition has been criticised in the more recent authorities. As Slade J

---

98 *O'Callaghan* v *Elliott* [1966] 1 QB 601.
99 For example, section 77 of the Railway Clauses Consolidation Act 1845 excludes mines and minerals from a conveyance of land unless they are expressly included in a conveyance of land conveyed under that Act.
1   See Chapter 1.
2   See *Davis* v *Shepherd* (1866) 1 Ch. App.410.
3   *O'Callaghan* v *Elliott* [1966] QB 601.

pointed out, in *Earl of Lonsdale* v *Attorney General*,[4] you cannot ignore the commercial context in which the grant or reservation took place. In that case the court had to construe an 1860 grant of the right to recover "mines and minerals" from land. The whole conveyance must be studied to see if the meaning is clear. Where it is not the court must look at the commercial background and commercial purpose in deciding what the parties true intentions were. On the facts of that case the phrase "mines and minerals" did not include oil and natural gas. In the context of an 1860 grant it would have been a reference to coal mines.

The word "mines", however, is clearly intended to refer to the extraction of underground minerals and does not refer to surface extraction which is more accurately referred to as "quarrying" than "mining".

---

4   [1982] 3 All ER 579.

CHAPTER 9
Resolving boundary disputes

Resolving boundary disputes

9.1
Self help

Although self help is not encouraged in most areas of contemporary English law in relation to land law it has continued to have some significance, for example, in relation to the forfeiture of a business lease. Here, I consider some of the miscellaneous rights of self-help that may be relevant in neighbour disputes even though the principal cause of the dispute is the correct boundary position.

It is well established that a neighbour may lop branches off a tree that overhangs his property,[5] but he cannot claim the expense from the owner of the tree. Such a right should not be exercised in a way that is disproportionate to the matter complained of and self-help ceases to be available when court action has been determined.[6]

In theory the owner of land has the right to remove a trespasser provided no more than reasonable force is used in doing so and that no violence is threatened.[7] However, this right is abrogated in the case of residential accommodation and it unlikely that many landowners would want to risk a trespass action if they are accused of using excessive force.

A further self help remedy that sometimes arises in conveyancing transactions is the remedy of rescission. Although a court may in certain circumstances order rescission of a contract, for example for misrepresentation, it is probably correctly classified as a self-help remedy.

The National Conditions of Sale (23rd Edition) provide[8] that in a contract for the sale of land to which those conditions apply rescission is available as a remedy in cases of fraud, recklessness or where the purchaser would be obliged but for rescission to purchase something

---

5   *Lemmon v Webb* [1895] AC 1 at 6.
6   *Burton v Winters* [1993] 1 WLR 1077.
7   Criminal Law Act 1977, section 6. For the position at common law see *Hemmings v Stoke Poges Golf Club* [1920] 1 KB 720.
8   Condition 7.1.3. For the rules on rescission generally see *Chitty on Contracts* 28th ed. vol. 1 e.g. at 6–101 et seq..

substantially different in quality or tenure from that which the error or omission had led him to expect he was to buy. Under those National Conditions either party may rescind.

However, at common law the right to rescind may be lost where *restitutio in integrum* is no longer possible. Where, for example, the innocent party has substantially used or altered the subject matter of the contract it is likely to be refused. Rescission will also be refused where the contract has been affirmed.[9]

Finally, a right of self-help also arises where a chattel is unlawfully left on land and has caused actual damage; i.e. the so-called right of damage feasant arises. The landowner may retain the chattel until the damage is paid for.

9.2
Court based litigation

An action for trespass, nuisance or for breach of a covenant for title in a conveyance is ultimately the way that boundary disputes may have to be resolved. A judgment following such a dispute operates *in personam* and is therefore strictly only binding on the parties.[10] In practice litigation is likely to resolve the dispute and result in a variation in the verbal description of the land or variation in the plan filed at the Land Registry and it would be difficult for a successor in title to revive a dispute settled between his predecessor in title and a neighbour, particularly having regard to the spirit if not the letter of the CPR.[11]

Where such an action is brought disclosure of relevant documents including documents of title is part of the process of litigation. Documents of title are admissible in any proceedings.[12]

The normal form of action by which the land is recovered is by ejectment proceedings but before such proceedings can succeed it is necessary to show title to the land in question. This will not necessarily

---

9   *Long* v *Lloyd* [1958] 2 All ER 402.
10 *Attorney General* v *Benyon* [1970] Ch 1 at 15.
11 See CPR 3.4.
12 Civil Evidence Act 1968, section 16, whereby the rule that a person who was not a party to civil proceedings could not be compelled to prove his title to any land was "abrogated" but in any event these documents are now normally admissible under section 9 of the Civil Evidence Act 1995, which applies to records of public authorities.

be a mere formality where there is a dispute over the correct boundary position.

Following the introduction of the Civil Procedure Rules (CPR) in 1999[13] litigation is no longer as much of a gladiatorial contest. The state now directs the gladiators and ensures that they have equality of arms with their quarries. It is no longer acceptable for the parties to litigate matters that are trivial and for the outcome to depend on the resources of the parties. The court now actively manages cases to ensure the real issues are identified and tried at the earliest opportunity in accordance with the overriding objective of trying cases justly.[14]

But whilst the reforms to the civil justice system introduced in 1999 seemed radical, and in many respects were radical, the changes have not been as great as was thought likely. For example, the principles of pleading established over many years are still relevant, although they are supplemented by the Rules in important respects. The recognition in the CPR of the need for a concise but complete statement of the nature of that party's case in the claim form[15] only reinforces the need for clarity in pleadings, which has been regarded as good pleading practice for many years.[16]

In land disputes the county court generally now has unlimited jurisdiction[17] but there are a number of specific exceptions, for example, in relation to a number of claims under the Law of Property Act 1925.[18] Subject to certain exceptions the county court may not award freezing orders (or Anton Pillar orders)[19] but otherwise has jurisdiction to grant injunctive or declaratory relief in all proceedings before it.[20] It may also award specific performance of a contractual obligation, as may the High Court. The equity limit of the county court remains £30,000 and has been since 1991.[21] But this is currently subject to review.[22]

---

13 They apply to all actions commenced after 26th April 1999 and applied to existing actions from the occasion of the first court date after that date.
14 CPR 1(1).
15 See CPR 16.4.
16 See Bullen and Leake's "Precedents of Pleadings", 14th ed., chapter 1.
17 See the High Court and County Court Jurisdiction Order 1991, art 1.
18 See article 1 (4) and (5) of the High Court and County Court Jurisdiction Order 1991, which place an upper financial limited on many such claims.
19 See County Court Remedies Regulations 1991 SI 1991/1222 (as amended by SI 1995/206), regulation 2, but the restriction does not apply to certain categories of case, for example those cases heard in the Central London Business List.
20 See County Courts Act 1984, section 38.
21 County Courts Jurisdiction Order 1981 IS 1981/1123.
22 See '*Modernising the Civil Courts – a Consultation Paper*' (January 2001).

In a money claim proceedings may only be commenced in the High Court where that claim has a financial value of more than £15,000.[23] In all other cases a claim may be brought in the county court where the financial value of the claim, the complexity of the facts, legal issues, remedies and procedures or the importance of the outcome for the public in general, justifies its commencement in the High Court.[24] The majority of boundary disputes will give rise to claims to money and to other types of relief and therefore it will be necessary to consider whether proceedings in the High Court are justified. Clearly, particularly in the Chancery Division, the parties are more likely to be allocated a judge of appropriate experience if the claim is issued in the High Court.

The CPR 16 Practice Direction contains guidance in relation to the form and content of statements of case. It permits a party to:

(1) Refer to any point of law;[25]
(2) Name any witness;[26]
(3) Attach a copy of any document considered necessary.[27]

In many boundary disputes it will be appropriate to set out in some detail the root of title and attach plans and other documents, which help to identify the nature and history of the dispute.

The power to strike out a case exists under the CPR as it existed under the old rules and summary judgment may entered on any claim or issue if there is no real prospect of that claim or issue succeeding.[28] In practice however summary judgment applications are rarer than under the old rules, not only because the wording is generally thought to be more onerous to applicants[29] for judgment but also because few weak cases get as far as the stage of issue. They tend to settle at the pre-issue negotiation stage, which is governed by an extensive regime of pre-action protocols.

Assuming the case proceeds as far as a trial (which rarely occurs since the CPR) it will be necessary to comply with the various directions that have been made together with the rules and practice

---

23 Article 4A of the High Court and County Court Jurisdiction Order.
24 PD 7A para 2.4.
25 CPR Pt 16 Practice Direction, Para 11.3(1) (see Para CPR PD 16).
26 CPR Pt 16 Practice Direction, paragraph 11.3(2) (see Para CPR PD 16).
27 CPR Pt 16 and the Practice Direction at para. 11.3 (3). It may include an expert's report (see CPR PD 16).
28 See CPR 3.4 and 24.
29 See *S v Gloucestershire CC* [2001] WLR 909.

directions which apply to the conduct of hearings. In particular Part 39 of the CPR and the Practice Direction thereto makes extensive provision for the conduct of and preparation for hearings.

The court may make directions that are appropriate to the case at various stages and this may include the lodging of bundles but in the absence of express provision it is the responsibility of the claimant to lodge a bundle of documents not more than seven not less than three days before the trial.[30] The bundle should include a case summary and/or chronology where appropriate, the witness statements (which should be in the form prescribed by CPR Part 32.8 and the Practice Direction that accompanies it), any notices of hearsay evidence that it is intended to rely on, any notice of the intention to rely on plans, photographs or models which are not contained in a witness statement under Part 33.6. Any experts' reports and responses to those reports should also be contained in the bundle together with any directions for the conduct of the trial. The contents of the bundle should be agreed wherever possible.

The guides to the various divisions of the High Court (for example the Chancery Guide) supplement in important respects the provisions of these rules and practice directions.

When the case gets to trial the judge will frequently not have looked at the case until the morning it is listed and may well have no prior knowledge of conveyancing, particularly in the county court. A case summary or chronology and preferably a skeleton argument is always helpful, even though under the Rules a skeleton argument is not required in the county court unless one is ordered. Appendix 3 to the Chancery Guide[31] describes the purpose of a skeleton argument as to "concisely summarise the parties submissions in relation to each of the issues... to cite the main authorities relied on. It is not the function of the skeleton argument to argue the case on paper". However, in my experience the skeleton argument is often the first thing the judge will read and it is therefore essential to have a simple summary of the facts and what the case is about. Few judges will in practice criticise a representative for treating them as though they know nothing about the case but no judges who know nothing about the case have ever been prepared to admit it!

At trial it is the invariable practice of the judge hearing a boundary dispute to have a site visit. These can either be at the start of the case or at the conclusion. Outside the formality of the court and given the

---

30 PD 39A paragraph 3.2.
31 In Volume 1 of the *Civil Court Practice*.

opportunity to say all the parties feel their representatives have failed to say over the course of the trial the litigants inevitably wish to tell the judge all sorts of irrelevant things that they believe will sway the case in their favour. This must be resisted by the judge and the legal representatives must guide their clients away from such comments because compliance with the rules of natural justice and Article 6 of the European Convention on Human Rights requires a formal fair and open trial process where each party can see clearly what the judge has or has not taken into account. The judge has to attach proper weight to the oral evidence at trial and cannot simply decide that the boundary is in a particular position from his own impressions formed on the site visit.[32] But in another case[33] it is clear that the recorder attached considerable weight to the site visit but the Court of Appeal nevertheless upheld his decision because it had been a proper one for him to reach in the circumstances.

9.3
The use of experts

Even in the less adversarial way in which litigation is conducted since the CPR were introduced, experts may be of considerable importance to resolving boundary disputes. They may also be of assistance where the parties do not resort to litigation and may be a cost effective way of resolving a boundary dispute. The parties may, for example, in the interests of saving time and money, refer a dispute to an expert surveyor and request an opinion by which they agree to be bound. Obviously in such a case it is particularly important to instruct a relevant expert who has no connection with the parties. This common sense requirement is replicated in the rules,[34] which govern the use of experts in court and in many cases reinforced by the professional codes of conduct under which experts practice.

The purpose of an expert is to provide technical or other expertise to assist the parties and the court to resolve disputes.[35] There has long

---

32 As occurred in *Charles v Beach* [1993] NPC 102.
33 *Horrod v Finney* [1992] NPC 145.
34 CPR Part 35.
35 See CPR Part 35, which provides a great deal of guidance on the duties of experts and the content of their reports.

been provision in the rules for court appointed experts[36] but in practice these are rare and in most cases the court will allow the parties to rely on a joint expert if it is necessary and proportionate. Exceptionally it will allow them to instruct an expert each.

The aim of the CPR was to reduce reliance on experts to cases where it was truly necessary and to reinforce the duties which experts had always had but were inclined to forget. In particular any expert owes a duty to the court to which he is required to provide his opinion and not to the party who employed him or who is responsible for his fee.

The litigant contemplating using an expert for court proceedings should ask whether an expert is necessary and if so to what issues his evidence is to be directed.[37] The inappropriate use of experts can lead to an increase in the costs of the litigation with no benefit to the parties or the court.

The expense of an expert must be proportionate to the issues in dispute in the litigation. The parties must make an assessment of the likely value of the claim and consider whether it is justified. The effect of this focus on cost in litigation is that responsible legal advice includes dispensing with the use of an expert where the cost is disproportionate to the issues, provided those issues can be resolved without instructing such an expert.

An expert must be truly independent of the parties and must be perceived to be so.[38] Even if, in a case management hearing, the court rules that an expert's evidence may be relied on, admissibility and weight are ultimately issues for the trial judge and where the expert appears not to have been truly impartial his evidence may be rejected or little weight attached to it.[39]

---

36 Such provision was first made as far back as 1934.

37 *Pozzolanic Lytag Ltd v Bryan Hobson Associates* (1998) 63 Con. LR 81 at 92 per Dyson J.

38 This requirement did not prevent a barrister, Mr Goldberg QC, recommending a colleague in chambers as an expert in litigation in which he was involved. The trial judge held that where there appears to be a relationship between one of the parties and the expert which a reasonable observer might conclude was capable of affecting his views, his evidence will not be admitted (Evans-Lombe J in *Liverpool Roman Catholic Archdiocesan Trustees Incorporated v Goldberg* (No. 3) [2001] 1WLR 2337, [2001] 4 All ER 950).

39 The case of *Field v Leeds City Council* [2000] 1 EGLR 54 illustrates the point. In that case Leeds City Council argued that one of their internal surveyors could provide the expert evidence in a housing disrepair case. Although the court concluded that he could, it is likely that there would be an issue as to the weight to be attached to that expert's evidence at the trial.

9.4
Arbitration

Arbitration may arise because there is an agreement in a contract or other instrument requiring that disputes are resolved in that way or because the parties are bound by virtue of the type of dispute that has arisen for it to be resolved by arbitration.

An "arbitration agreement" is defined as "an agreement to submit to arbitration present or future disputes (whether they are contractual or not)"[40] and any clause to this effect will be binding. Therefore a claim in tort may be referred to arbitration for resolution. Commercial leases frequently contain a clause to the effect that all disputes shall be referred to arbitration and this would include disputes over party structures and divisions. A court has power to stay proceedings brought in contravention of such a clause.[41] CPR Part 62 sets out the procedure by which a reference to arbitration may be invoked.

In a boundary dispute a reference to arbitration is most likely to occur where the disputants occupy land under a commercial lease. But a reference to arbitration may also occur under various statutes, for example, under section 84 of the Agricultural Holdings Act 1986, and this may include arbitration as to the boundary of a holding within that Act.[42]

As we shall see in the next section, dispute resolution clauses are increasingly common, but it has been held that these do not entitle a party to a stay as would occur in the case of an arbitration clause.[43] However, such clauses may have an important effect on the exercise of the court's discretion on costs.

---

40 Arbitration Act 1996, section 6(1).
41 Arbitration Act 1996, section 9.
42 See for example *Secretary of State for Defence* v *Spencer* [2002] NPC 128.
43 *Halifax Financial Services Limited* v *Intuitive Systems Limited* [1999] 1 All ER (Comm.) 303.

9.5
Alternative dispute resolution

ADR is increasingly seen both as an alternative to conventional court-based dispute resolution and as a compliment to the traditional system. As the *Admiralty and Commercial Court Guide*[44] indicates:[45]

> "Legal representatives should in all cases consider with their clients and the other parties concerned the possibility of attempting to resolve the dispute or particular issues by ADR and should ensure their clients are informed of the most cost effective means of resolving their dispute."

The advantages are well known; ADR is less costly, it is confidential and, particularly in a dispute between neighbours, has the advantage of retaining a working relationship between the parties. Its disadvantage is that in an inappropriate case it may increase costs and delay justice. Where a client has a strong legal argument in his favour it may be inappropriate to ignore that argument and refer the matter to ADR.

The CPR encourages the use of ADR in CPR 26.4. That is in accordance with the overriding objective of ensuring that the parties are on an equal footing and that costs are proportionate to the issues.[46] The Access to Justice Report in 1995 made clear its commitment to these concepts and the current edition of the CPR make reference to ADR in CPR 1.4(2)(e).

That rule provides that "actively managing cases" includes:

> "Encouraging the parties to use an alternative dispute resolution procedure if the court considers that to be appropriate and facilitating the use of such procedure."

It will be noted that each of the specialist court guides encourage the use of ADR.

As well as the encouraging the use of ADR as an alternative to the trial process contained in the CPR (indeed not to do so can place the parties and their advisers in danger of adverse costs consequences[47]) the Court of Appeal has encouraged its use at the appeal stage since 1997 and has its own mediation scheme.

---

44 The current edition of which is found in the *Civil Court Practice 2002*.
45 At paragraph G1.4.
46 CPR 1.1(1)–(2).
47 *Dunnett v Railtrack PLC (in railway administration)* [2002] All ER (D) 314.

The Admiralty and Commercial Court Guide[48] indicates[49] the range of orders available where cases before that court are referred to mediation and therefore provides some guidance in other cases not before that court. They include provision for the selection of a mediator, and an order to the effect that the parties are required to take serious steps towards resolving their differences by ADR, failing which the matter must be referred back to court for it to exercise its further case management powers.

Sometimes the reference to ADR may be accommodated within the existing timetable. Alternatively it is open to the court to provide for an adjournment or a stay "for ADR to take place", but this type of order is likely to be rare.[50] The court will normally make provision for further orders to be made at the case management stage if the stay does not produce the desired settlement.

Section 4(4) of the Access to Justice Act 1999 provides for public funding to be available for the mediation of non-family civil claims. Mediation fees and expenses may be treated as disbursements and lawyers fees for preparation treated as ordinary preparation costs. However, boundary disputes are excluded from the scheme.[51]

ADR may take a number of different forms but commonly mediation is used. Either the mediator facilitates the parties to effectively negotiate a settlement in a controlled environment or the mediator may be required to express a view on the rights or wrongs of the case, in which case he will require specialist knowledge of the law and technical background to the dispute. Which method of mediation is chosen will depend on the extent to which the parties wish to be bound by the mediation and the nature of their dispute.

---

48 Found in the *Civil Court Practice 2002* in volume 1.

49 In Appendix 7.

50 The more usual remedy was for the court to provide a more spaced out case management timetable to enable ADR to take place (see *Cable and Wireless plc* v *IBM UK Limited* [2002] All ER (D) 277).

51 By section 6 (6) and Schedule 2 of the Access to Justice Act 1999. However, claims to harrassment may be within the funding code.

CHAPTER 10
Court based remedies and orders

Court based remedies and orders

10.1
Injunctions

Introduction

An injunction is available where damages are an inadequate remedy. It has been described as a flexible remedy, which flows from its equitable character.[52] Because the court's jurisdiction is equitable in character the claimant must have clean hands and where the relief sought is urgent the claimant must act accordingly. The courts of equity that developed the remedy of the injunction also developed the doctrines of laches and acquiescence. These doctrines can prevent the claimant obtaining this most useful form of equitable relief, particularly where an interim or interlocutory injunction is claimed.[53]

There are a large variety of injunctions available but those of greatest relevance to this area are interlocutory or interim injunctions, which are imposed to prohibit the defendant from continuing with a course of action which infringes the claimant's legal rights until the trial. These are separately considered below.

Most injunctions are prohibitory in character but occasionally the courts are asked to impose mandatory injunctions which compel the defendant, for example, to remove an offending structure from the claimant's land.

Where the claimant seeks a mandatory interlocutory injunction different considerations will apply and the onus of showing that the claimant has acted with due expedition will be all the stronger. Generally the courts are more reluctant to grant a mandatory

---

52 See *Spry on Equitable Remedies* 3rd ed. at p.380 and Snell '*Principles of Equity*' 30th ed. at p.713.
53 Present terminology is to refer to "interim injunctions" (see CPR 25.1) however the term "interlocutory injunction" will be used throughout this chapter because many of the cases use the old terminology.

interlocutory injunction than a prohibitory interlocutory injunction. In particular, in addition to the requirements that must be satisfied before any interlocutory injunction will be granted the court will require a high degree of assurance that the claimant will succeed at trial.[54] The court will be concerned to balance the injustice to the defendant if it turns out that the injunction was wrongly imposed against the injustice to the claimant of perhaps suffering irreparable damage.[55]

In the classic formulation by Smith LJ in *Shelfer* v *City of London Electric Lighting Company*[56] in deciding whether to grant an injunction the court would consider the following in deciding whether or not to exercise its discretion in favour of the applicant:

"(1) If the injury to the plaintiff's legal rights is small,

(2) And is capable of being estimated in money,

(3) And is one capable of being compensated by a small money payment,

(4) And the case is one in which it would be oppressive to the defendant to grant an injunction: –

Then damages in substitution for an injunction may be given.

There may also be cases in which, though the four above-mentioned requirements exist, the defendant by his conduct, as for instance hurrying up a building so as if possible to avoid an injunction or otherwise acting with a reckless disregard to the plaintiff's rights, has disentitled himself from asking that damages may be assessed in substitution for an injunction."

There are, however, certain recognised categories of cases where an injunction will invariably be refused:

---

54 *Shepherd Homes Limited* v *Sandham* [1971] 1 Ch.340.
55 See *Nottingham Building Society* v *Eurodynamics* [1993] FSR 474, in which Chadwick J authoritatively stated the principles to apply to interlocutory mandatory injunctions. Chadwick J's judgment was expressely approved by the Court of Appeal in *Zockoll Group Ltd* v *Mercury Communications Ltd* [1998] FSR 354.
56 [1895] 1 Ch. 287 at 323.

Where damages are an adequate remedy

The court will consider first and foremost whether damages are an adequate remedy.[57] Damages will be considered an adequate remedy where the damage is trivial or where the damage done by the imposition of an injunction is disproportionate to the benefit to be derived by the claimant.[58]

In *Wrotham Park Estates* v *Parkside Homes* [1974] 1 WLR 798 the claimants delayed in applying for an interlocutory injunction until after some houses had been built on land which was subject to a restrictive covenant. In the circumstances the court refused them a mandatory injunction at trial to compel the removal of the offending structures. One of the reasons the Court of Appeal gave was that to compel the removal of the houses concerned would involve an "unpardonable waste of much needed houses". Therefore the order would not be made.

Where there has been excessive delay

Excessive delay is an important factor in deciding whether to grant or refuse an injunction, particularly where an interlocutory injunction is sought, but delay in itself will rarely justify refusal. The delay must be such as to indicate acquiescence on the part of the claimant which makes the grant of an injunction unconscionable.

In *Jones* v *Stones*[59] the Court of Appeal allowed an appeal against a finding that three years delay constituted acquiescence on the part of the claimant. As has been pointed out delay in itself will not justify a refusal of relief on grounds of acquiescence. It must be asked whether there was any action or inaction on the part of the claimant which justified the belief on the part of the defendant that he was entitled to proceed with the action of the type the injunction was designed to prevent. Secondly, it must be asked whether it would be unconscionable to allow the claimant to assert his strict legal rights. On the facts of that case there was no detrimental reliance on any acts or omissions of the claimant and hence the plea of acquiescence failed.

---

57 See *Jaggard* v *Sawyer* [1995] 1WLR 270.
58 *Shepherd Homes Ltd* v *Sandham* (*supra*) and see also *Ketley* v *Gooden* (1996) 73 P&CR 305.
59 [1999] 1 WLR 1739.

However, in *Jaggard* v *Sawyer*[60] the claimant delayed in bringing an application for an injunction to restrain a neighbour from carrying out development in breach of a restrictive covenant and indeed failed altogether to apply for an interlocutory injunction. It was held by the Court of Appeal that the failure to apply for an interlocutory injunction coupled with the relatively minor impact on the visual amenity of the claimant's house meant that the grant of a perpetual injunction to restrain development was inappropriate. The court therefore assessed damages under section 50 of the Supreme Court Act based on the amount the claimant could reasonably have insisted upon for relaxation of the covenant and not a ransom price.

It is thus the practice of the courts to refuse injunctive relief at trial in any case where the claimant has stood by whilst a breach of his legal rights has occurred, particularly in cases where it would be oppressive to impose an injunction. This will invariably be so where a building or structure has been erected at substantial cost[61] to the defendant. But it is a matter of degree whether actions of the claimant would become oppressive. Clearly many clients will be reluctant to take on a substantial developer where they must give an undertaking as to damages, something which is likely to cause all but the exceedingly rich to pause.

The court's power to grant an injunction

The jurisdiction of the High Court to award an injunction is derived from section 37 of the Supreme Court Act 1981. The county court's jurisdiction is derived from section 38 of the County Courts Act 1984 and the County Court Remedies Regulations 1991.[62] In the county court any judge may grant an injunction but subject to some minor exceptions[63] only a High Court judge may grant a freezing type injunction or an injunction which includes relief of that type.

In addition to the court's general power to award an injunction under the above provisions, since the commencement of the Protection from Harassment Act 1997[64] the court has a specific power to impose

---

60 [1995] 1 WLR 269.
61 *Jaggard* v *Sawyer* (*supra*) and *Gafford* v *Graham* [1999] 3 EGLR 75.
62 SI 1991/1222.
63 *Supra*.
64 On 16th June 1997.

an injunction where the offending party is guilty of harassment. "Harassment" is defined by section 1 as:

"(1) ... A course of conduct—

(a) Which amounts to harassment of another, and

(b) Which he knows or ought to know amounts to harassment of the other.

(2) For the purposes of this section, the person whose course of conduct is in question ought to know that it amounts to harassment of another if a reasonable person in possession of the same information would think the course of conduct amounted to harassment of the other."

The Act, which contains both civil and criminal sanctions together with a power of arrest in certain circumstances, may be added to a claim for nuisance or trespass. In addition to its wider sanctions it has the further advantage that claims under the Act may qualify for Legal Services Commission Funding whereas boundary disputes do not.

Where proceedings are commenced under the Act they should comply with Part 8 of the CPR.

Interlocutory injunctions – the American Cyanamid principles

As we have seen speed is of the essence when applying for injunctions and this is particularly so in relation to interlocutory injunctions.

It has been well established since the case of *American Cyanamid* v *Ethicon*[65] that the following requirements must be met before the court will grant an interlocutory prohibitory injunction, which provides a helpful checklist:

1) There must be a serious issue to be tried;

2) Damages must be an inadequate remedy;

3) The balance of convenience should favour the grant of such relief;

4) The claimant must be able to compensate the defendant for any loss he may suffer if the injunction is subsequently discharged.

---

65 [1975] AC 396.

The claimant will be expected to make full and frank disclosure to the court in order to obtain an interlocutory injunction and this will extend to disclosing information that is harmful to his case. The requirement of having "clean hands" extends to showing that the action proposed by the defendant must constitute a real infringement of the claimant's legal rights and must not be merely petty in character.[66] On the other hand, in an appropriate case the court may grant the claimant everything he would have obtained at trial, indeed, it may be seen as furthering the overriding objective in Part 1 of the CPR for the court to do so.

In an appropriate case the claimant may claim an interlocutory injunction prior to issuing his claim form.[67]

10.2
Damages

A claimant who establishes that a trespass has taken place is entitled to damages whether or not he is also entitled to an injunction since trespass (as opposed to the tort of private nuisance, where some damage must be proved but some may be presumed) is actionable *per se* but that is not to say that every trespass however trivial will attract substantial damages. Where it is alleged that the claimant has suffered a quantifiable loss, for example, the cost of reinstating a boundary structure, he must plead the cost and prove that he will expend the damages he is awarded on reinstatement.[68] Thus, in *Hole & Son (Sayers Common) v Harrison of Thurnscoe*[69] no substantial damages were awarded because the court concluded that the claimant was likely to demolish the outbuilding with which the case was concerned and could not therefore have the cost of building a replacement by way of damages. Those damages would only result in a windfall to him.

In many cases where the owner is effectively ousted from part of his land he is entitled to mesne profits for the market rent of the land unlawfully occupied for the period of occupation. Where the trespasser has derived a profit from his unlawful occupation the court may

---

66 *Tollemache & Cobold Breweries Limited* v *Reynolds* (1983) 268 EG 52.
67 CPR 25.2.
68 Indeed it is still a principle of pleading that any claim to special damages must be properly particularised and proved (see *Ilkiw* v *Samuels* [1963] 1 WLR 991).
69 [1973] 1 Ll. R 345.

deprive him of that profit. In addition the owner can claim the cost of reinstating the land to its former condition.

Where the breach is substantial the courts will award substantial amounts, sometimes at a daily amount to encourage the defendant to restore the *status quo*. Thus in *Ryan & Ryan v AL Harwood Building Services*[70] A had been instructed by Rs' neighbour to build an extension to his house right up to the edge of his land. The extension was built immediately abutting Rs' property, in particular the garage and kitchen extension, which were flat roofed extensions and only one storey high. The building works took approximately three months during the summer of 1994. The Rs went on holiday and returned to find that A had constructed scaffolding, without their consent, on their kitchen and garage roofs. Despite being asked to take it down immediately, A delayed matters for a further four days. Further, throughout the period of the building works builders would be on R's kitchen and garage roofs, without consent, attending to the construction of the neighbour's extension.

The judge relied on the Court of Appeal decision in *Whitwham v Westminster Brymbo Coal and Coke Co*[71] and held that the damages for trespass should be assessed upon the wayleave principles. In essence, the measure of damages was assessed by reference to what hypothetically might have been agreed as a charge for the use of Rs' land. In particular, the judge found that he should take account of what would have been Rs' extremely strong bargaining position given that A had already contracted to build the extension for the neighbour. The judge awarded £125 per day for the period the scaffolding was on the roof, which was a total of 21 days, and £20 per day for the period the rest of the building work was continuing and the roof being used daily by the builders, a total of 60 days.

Damages can also be awarded in substitution for an injunction under section 50 of the Supreme Court Act 1981 (section 38 of the County Courts Act 1984). The jurisdiction under those Acts extends to compensating the claimant for future wrongs and not merely, as at common law, compensating the claimant for past damage.

Damages in the *Wrotham Park* case (*supra*) were assessed on the basis of the amount the claimants could legitimately have demanded of the defendants for relaxing the restrictive covenant in question. It is

---

70 Central London County Court, Judge Dean, November 22nd 1996, (1997 CLY 1775).
71 [1896] 2 Ch. 538.

clear from the *Sandham* case[72] that the claimant may not "name his price", a point which is sometimes overlooked in boundary cases involving a "ransom strip", but, as in *Wrotham Park*, a percentage of the profit could legitimately be asked for (in that case 5% of the anticipated profit).

Where someone if forcibly removed from his land and actual violence is used or threatened the owner of the land may be entitled in tort to aggravated damages. These damages are punitive rather than compensatory in character and are supposed to reflect the court's opprobrium for the actions of the trespasser. Similarly, in tort, exemplary damages may be awarded in the exceptional case where a trespass has been committed after the tortfeasor has calculated that the profit to be made from his unlawful actions exceeds the likely compensation he would be liable to pay if he pursued the other party through proper legal channels. Where the tortfeasor has "cocked a snook" at the court in this way the court will do the same to him by penalising him, normally, with a significant lump sum award. However such cases are rare in the area of neighbour disputes but they are routinely awarded in residential unlawful eviction cases.[73]

At the opposite extreme nominal damages are sometimes awarded where the loss claimed is so small that it is incapable of calculation.[74] Such damages (frequently in the sum of £5 or less) will also be awarded where the claimant has effectively lost his claim. Outside the field of libel, where this frequently occurs, such awards occur in boundary disputes where a right to land is established which is not of substance.[75]

Obviously, any claim for damages in tort is subject to the normal rules on causation and remoteness.[76]

---

72 [1971] 1 Ch. 340.
73 For the principles, particularly in the housing context, see *Drane* v *Evangelou* [1978] 1 WLR 455.
74 As occurred in the case of *Nelson* v *Nicholson* '*The Independent*' 22/1/01, CA.
75 See *Mc Gregor on Damages* 16th ed. chapter 10.
76 See *Overseas Tankship (UK)* v *Miller Steamship Co Pty (the Wagon Mound (No. 2))* [1967] 1 AC 617.

10.3
Declarations

Provided the court has jurisdiction to hear the case it may grant a declaration as a freestanding remedy. The county courts' jurisdiction to grant declaratory relief does not depend on the existence of a claim for money,[77] and in some cases it will be the only form of relief sought. In an appropriate case an interim declaration may be granted[78] although this is rare in practice.

The High Court has the power to declare any legislation incompatible with the European Convention on Human Rights. But although there have been some challenges in this area, they are unlikely to frequent.[79]

10.4
Costs

The claimant who succeeds in establishing his legal title to land will wish to recover as much of his costs as possible if the victory is not to be a hollow one. The introduction of the CPR has reduced the volume of litigation and completely changed the way that costs are incurred away from the litigation process to the pre-action stage.

Once the courts realised that the changes in the costs regime were of substance they began to use their new powers, which are principally contained in three rules and practice directions,[80] with enthusiasm. A disproportionate use of the court's time, litigating about the matters which are not of true substance, particularly in a disproportionately drawn out trial procedure, and failing to protect the position of the litigant by making appropriate offers to settle and or payments

---

77 See for example *Osei-Bonsu* v *Wandsworth London Borough Council* [1999] 1 All ER 265, [1999] 1 WLR 1011, CA.

78 See CPR 25.1.

79 See *Poplar Housing Regeneration and Community Association Limited* v *Donoghue* [2001] 3 WLR 183.

80 They are contained principally in Parts 43, 44 and 48 but there are no less than five other provisions, whereas under the Rules of the Supreme Court they were contained in just one (Order 62). However to make matters more complicated the practitioner also needs to have regard to the provisions of the various practice directions made pursuant to those rules.

into court, will all provoke the use of the court's swingeing new costs sanctions.[81]

The court's discretion is wider under the CPR than under the former rules and the premium on good advice is therefore much greater. Predicting the outcome of a costs argument in a neighbour dispute is particularly difficult but often particularly important for the client.

Costs are normally awarded on a standard basis, i.e. they are limited to such costs as are proportionate to the matters in issue and any doubt as to whether they were reasonable and proportionate in amount will be resolved in favour of the paying party.[82] But as we shall see, in certain circumstances costs may be awarded on an indemnity basis.[83]

Protection of the client's position on costs

The principal method of protecting the client is to make a payment into court or offer to settle under the provisions of Part 36 CPR. In a money claim the defendant should make a Part 36 payment where he wishes to protect his position on costs.[84] Where there is both a money claim and a non-money claim, as is likely to be the case in a boundary dispute, the defendant should make an offer to settle the non-money part of the claim together with a Part 36 payment.[85]

The current rules also allow a claimant may make a Part 36 offer at any stage provided it is made "not less than 21 days before the trial".[86] Where an offer (or in the case of a defendant, a payment) is made less than 21 days before the trial it should state that the offeree may accept it if the parties agree liability for costs or the court gives permission.

Where a Part 36 offer or payment is accepted within the time allowed by the rules (i.e. 21 days) the offeree is entitled to his costs up to the date of serving a notice of acceptance.[87] Where a claimant fails to "do better" than the amount paid into court or to gain a "more advantageous" judgment[88] the paying or offering party is entitled to his costs for the period after the time allowed for acceptance unless the

---

81 See e.g. *SCT Finance* v *Bolton* [2002] All ER (D) 75.
82 Part 44.4(2).
83 Part 44.4(3).
84 Part 36.3.
85 Part 39.4(2).
86 Part 36.5(6).
87 Part 36.13.
88 Part 36.20.

court considers it "unjust to do so". A claimant who does better than the payment into court or obtains a more advantageous outcome is normally entitled to his costs. However where the claimant does better than the amount of his own Part 36 offer the extraordinary swingeing powers under Part 36.21 apply. In particular he is entitled to costs on an indemnity basis and to interest on any judgment debt at 10% above the base rate. Although the rule says the court "may" make these orders it goes on to state that "may" means "will" "unless it considers it unjust to do so". It is difficult to see how it can be just to award a claimant a rate of interest above any commercial rate of return simply because he happens to guess the correct figure for damages. In boundary disputes, as we have seen, this figure is to an even greater extent a matter of guesswork than in other cases.

In practice the award of costs is likely to be more complex in boundary disputes and in particular the court is likely to exercise its wide discretion to award or not to award costs based on the wide range of factors in Part 44.5 CPR. Those include the value of the property involved and the conduct before as well as during the litigation.

10.5
Conditional fees

Conditional fees are likely to become of greater practical significance in neighbour disputes than they are now. The Access to Justice Act 1999 provides[89] that the costs of insuring the opposing side's costs and the success fee may be recovered from the unsuccessful defendant and the Court of Appeal have given guidance on the extent to which an "uplift" agreed in advance of the litigation may be recovered from the unsuccessful defendant.[90]

Experience so far (which, as the House of Lords acknowledged in *Callery* v *Gray*,[91] was not substantial) has shown the unpredictability of outcomes in litigation in which conditional fee agreements have been entered into. Although there is more likely to be a "right answer" to a dispute concerning a party wall than in a personal injury claim, it is unlikely that conditional fee agreements will be widely used in

---

89 In Part II.
90 *Callery* v *Gray* [2001] 1 WLR 2142.
91 [2002] 1 WLR 2000.

this type of litigation, therefore. At this stage there is little useful guidance which specifically relates to this type of litigation as opposed to litigation generally.

Appendices

Appendix 1
Statutory and other extracts

Law of Property Act 1925, sections 53, 62 and 205

53 Instruments required to be in writing

(1) Subject to the provisions hereinafter contained with respect to the creation of interests in land by parol—

(a) no interest in land can be created or disposed of except by writing signed by the person creating or conveying the same, or by his agent thereunto lawfully authorised in writing, or by will, or by operation of law;

(b) a declaration of trust respecting any land or any interest therein must be manifested and proved by some writing signed by some person who is able to declare such trust or by his will;

(c) a disposition of an equitable interest or trust subsisting at the time of the disposition, must be in writing signed by the person disposing of the same, or by his agent thereunto lawfully authorised in writing or by will.

(2) This section does not affect the creation or operation of resulting, implied or constructive trusts.

62 General words implied in conveyances

(1) A conveyance of land shall be deemed to include and shall by virtue of this Act operate to convey, with the land, all buildings, erections, fixtures, commons, hedges, ditches, fences, ways, waters, watercourses, liberties, privileges, easements, rights, and advantages whatsoever, appertaining or reputed to appertain to the land, or any part thereof, or, at the time of conveyance, demised, occupied, or enjoyed with or reputed or known as part or parcel of or appurtenant to the land or any part thereof.

(2) A conveyance of land, having houses or other buildings thereon, shall be deemed to include and shall by virtue of this Act operate to convey, with the land, houses, or other buildings, all outhouses, erections, fixtures, cellars, areas, courts, courtyards, cisterns, sewers, gutters, drains, ways, passages, lights, watercourses, liberties, privileges, easements, rights, and advantages whatsoever, appertaining or reputed to appertain to the land, houses, or other buildings conveyed, or any of them, or any part thereof, or, at the time of conveyance,

demised, occupied, or enjoyed with, or reputed or known as part or parcel of or appurtenant to, the land, houses, other buildings conveyed, or any of them, or any part thereof.

(3) A conveyance of a manor shall be deemed to include and shall by virtue of this Act operate to convey, with the manor, all pastures, feedings, wastes, warrens, commons, mines, minerals, quarries, furzes, trees, woods, underwoods, coppices, and the ground and soil thereof, fishings, fisheries, fowlings, courts leet, courts baron, and other courts, view of frankpledge and all that to view of frankpledge doth belong, mills, mulctures, customs, tolls, duties, reliefs, heriots, fines, sums of money, amerciaments, waifs, estrays, chief-rents, quitrents, rentscharge, rents seck, rents of assize, fee farm rents, services, royalties, jurisdictions, franchises, liberties, privileges, easements, profits, advantages, rights, emoluments, and hereditaments whatsoever, to the manor appertaining or reputed to appertain, or, at the time of conveyance, demised, occupied, or enjoyed with the same, or reputed or known as part, parcel, or member thereof.

For the purposes of this subsection the right to compensation for manorial incidents of the extinguishment thereof shall be deemed to be a right appertaining to the manor.

(4) This section applies only if and as far as a contrary intention is not expressed in the conveyance, and has effect subject to the terms of the conveyance and to the provisions therein contained.

(5) This section shall not be construed as giving to any person a better title to any property, right, or thing in this section mentioned than the title which the conveyance gives to him to the land or manor expressed to be conveyed, or as conveying to him any property, right, or thing in this section mentioned, further or otherwise than as the same could have been conveyed to him by the conveying parties.

(6) This section applies to conveyances made after the thirty-first day of December, eighteen hundred and eighty-one.

205 General definitions

(1) In this Act unless the context otherwise requires, the following expressions have the meanings hereby assigned to them respectively, that is to say:—

    (i)   "Bankruptcy" includes liquidation by arrangement; also in relation to a corporation means the winding up thereof;

(ii)   "Conveyance" includes a mortgage, charge, lease, assent, vesting declaration, vesting instrument, disclaimer, release and every other assurance of property or of an interest therein by any instrument, except a will; "convey" has a corresponding meaning; and "disposition" includes a conveyance and also a devise, bequest, or an appointment of property contained in a will; and "dispose of" has a corresponding meaning;

(iii) "Building purposes" include the erecting and improving of, and the adding to, and the repairing of buildings; and a "building lease" is a lease for building purposes or purposes connected therewith;

[(iiiA) ...]

(iv)   "Death duty" means estate duty, ... and every other duty leviable or payable on a death;

(v)   "Estate owner" means the owner of a legal estate, but an infant is not capable of being an estate owner;

(vi)   "Gazette" means the London Gazette;

(vii) "Incumbrance" includes a legal or equitable mortgage and a trust for securing money, and a lien, and a charge of a portion, annuity or other capital or annual sum; and "incumbrancer" has a meaning corresponding with that of incumbrance, and includes every person entitled to the benefit of an incumbrance, or to require payment or discharge thereof;

(viii) "Instrument" does not include a statute, unless the statute creates a settlement;

(ix)   "Land" includes land of any tenure, and mines and minerals, whether or not held apart from the surface, buildings or parts of buildings (whether the division is horizontal, vertical or made in any other way) and other corporeal hereditaments; also a manor, an advowson, and a rent and other incorporeal hereditaments, and an easement, right, privilege, or benefit in, over, or derived from land; *but not an undivided share in land*; and "mines and minerals" include any strata or seam of minerals or substances in or under any land, and powers of working and getting the same *but not an undivided share thereof*; and "manor" includes a lordship, and reputed manor or lordship; and "hereditament" means any real property which on an intestacy occurring before the commencement of this Act might have devolved upon an heir;

(x) "Legal estates" mean the estates, interests and charges, in or over land (subsisting or created at law) which are by this Act authorised to subsist or to be created as legal estates; "equitable interests" mean all the other interests and charges in or over land *or in the proceeds of sale thereof*; an equitable interest "capable of subsisting as a legal estate" means such as could validly subsist or be created as a legal estate under this Act;

(xi) "Legal powers" include the powers vested in a chargee by way of legal mortgage or in an estate owner under which a legal estate can be transferred or created; and "equitable powers" mean all the powers in or over land under which equitable interests or powers only can be transferred or created;

(xii) "Limitation Acts" means the Real Property Limitation Acts 1833, 1837 and 1874, and "limitation" includes a trust;

[(xiii) "Mental disorder" has the meaning assigned to it by [section 1 of the Mental Health Act 1983] and "receiver" in relation to a person suffering from mental disorder, means a receiver appointed for that person under [Part VIII of the Mental Health Act 1959 or Part VII of the said Act of 1983].]

(xiv) a "mining lease" means a lease for mining purposes, that is, the searching for, winning, working, getting, making merchantable, carrying away, or disposing of mines and minerals, or purposes connected therewith, and includes a grant or licence for mining purposes;

(xv) "Minister" means [the Minister of Agriculture, Fisheries and Food];

(xvi) "Mortgage" includes any charge or lien on any property for securing money or money's worth; "legal mortgage" means a mortgage by demise or subdemise or a charge by way of legal mortgage and "legal mortgagee" has a corresponding meaning; "mortgage money" means money or money's worth secured by a mortgage; "mortgagor" includes any person from time to time deriving title under the original mortgagor or entitled to redeem a mortgage according to his estate interest or right in the mortgaged property; "mortgagee" includes a chargee by way of legal mortgage and any person from time to time deriving title under the original mortgagee; and "mortgagee in possession" is, for the purposes of this Act, a mortgagee who, in right of the mortgage, has entered into and is in possession of the mortgaged property; and "right of redemption" includes an option to repurchase only if the option in effect creates a right of redemption;

(xvii)   "Notice" includes constructive notice;

(xviii) "Personal representative" means the executor, original or by representation, or administrator for the time being of a deceased person, and as regards any liability for the payment of death duties includes any person who takes possession of or intermeddles with the property of a deceased person without the authority of the personal representatives or the court;

(xix)   "Possession" includes receipt of rents and profits or the right to receive the same, if any; and "income" includes rents and profits;

(xx)   "Property" includes any thing in action, and any interest in real or personal property;

(xxi)   "Purchaser" means a purchaser in good faith for valuable consideration and includes a lessee, mortgagee or other person who for valuable consideration acquires an interest in property except that in Part I of this Act and elsewhere where so expressly provided "purchaser" only means a person who acquires an interest in or charge on property for money or money's worth; and in reference to a legal estate includes a chargee by way of legal mortgage; and where the context so requires "purchaser" includes an intending purchaser; "purchase" has a meaning corresponding with that of "purchaser; and "valuable consideration" includes marriage but does not include a nominal consideration in money;

(xxii)   "Registered land" has the same meaning as in the Land Registration Act 1925, and "Land Registrar" means the Chief Land Registrar under that Act;

(xxiii) "Rent" includes a rent service or a rentcharge, or other rent, toll, duty, royalty, or annual or periodical payment in money or money's worth, reserved or issuing out of or charged upon land, but does not include mortgage interest; "rentcharge" includes a fee farm rent; "fine" includes a premium or foregift and any payment, consideration, or benefit in the nature of a fine, premium or foregift; "lessor" includes an underlessor and a person deriving title under a lessor or underlessor; and "lessee" includes an underlessee and a person deriving title under a lessee or underlessee, and "lease" includes and underlease or other tenancy;

(xxiv) "Sale" includes an extinguishment of manorial incidents, but in other respects means a sale properly so called;

(xxv) "Securities" include stocks, funds and shares

(xxvi) "Tenant for life", "statutory owner", "settled land", "settlement", "vesting deed", "subsidiary vesting deed", "vesting order", "vesting instrument", "trust instrument", "capital money" and "trustees of the settlement" have the same meanings as in the Settled Land Act 1925;

(xxvii) "Term of years absolute" means a term of years (taking effect either in possession or in reversion whether or not at a rent) with or without impeachment for waste, subject or not to another legal estate, and either certain or liable to determination by notice, re-entry, operation of law, or by a provision for cesser on redemption or in any other event (other than the dropping of a life, or the determination of a determinable life interest); but does not include any term of years determinable with life or lives or with the ??? of a determinable life interest, nor, if created after the commencement of this Act, a term of years which is not expressed to take effect in possession within twenty-one years after the creation thereof where required by this Act to take effect within that period; and in this definition the expression "term of years" includes a term for less than a year, or for a year or years and a fraction of a year or from year to year;

(xxviii) "Trust Corporation" means the Public Trustee or a corporation either appointed by the court in any particular case to be a trustee or entitled by rules made under subsection (3) of section four of the Public Trustee Act 1906 to act as custodian trustee;

(xxix) "Trust for sale", in relation to land, means an immediate *binding* trust for sale, whether or not exercisable at the request or with the consent of any person, and with or without a power at discretion to postpone the sale; "trustees for sale" mean the persons (including a personal representative) holding land on trust for sale; *and "power to postpone a sale" means power to postpone in the exercise of a discretion*;

(xxx) "United Kingdom" means Great Britain and Northern Ireland;

(xxxi) "Will" includes codicil.

[(1A) Any reference in this Act to money being paid into court shall be construed as referring to the money being paid into the Supreme Court or any other court that has jurisdiction, and any reference in this Act to the court, in a context referring to the investment or application of money paid into court, shall be construed, in the case of money paid into the Supreme Court, as referring to the High Court, and in the case of money paid into another court, as referring to that other court.]

(2) Where an equitable interest in or power over property arises by statute or operation of law, references to the creation of an interest or power include references to any interest or power so arising.

(3) References to registration under the Land Charges Act 1925 apply to any registration made under any other statute which is by the Land Charges Act 1925 to have effect as if the registration had been made under that Act.

Land Registration Act 1925, sections 75, 76, 82 and 110

75 Acquisition of title by possession

(1) The Limitation Acts shall apply to registered land in the same manner and to the same extent as those Acts apply to land not registered, except that where, if the land were not registered, the estate of the person registered as proprietor would be extinguished, such estate shall not be extinguished but shall be deemed to be held by the proprietor for the time being in trust for the person who, by virtue of the said Acts, has acquired title against any proprietor, but without prejudice to the estates and interests of any other person interested in the land whose estate or interest is not extinguished by those Acts.

(2) Any person claiming to have acquired a title under the Limitation Acts to a registered estate in the land may apply to be registered as proprietor thereof.

(3) The registrar shall, on being satisfied as to the applicant's title, enter the applicant as proprietor either with absolute, good leasehold, qualified, or possessory title, as the case may require, but without prejudice to any estate or interest protected by any entry on the register which may not have been extinguished under the Limitation Acts, and such registration shall, subject as aforesaid, have the same effect as the registration of a first proprietor; but the proprietor or the applicant or any other person interested may apply to the court for the determination of any question arising under this section.

(4) ...

(5) Rules may be made for applying (subject to any necessary modifications) the provisions of this section to cases where an easement, right or privilege has been acquired by prescription.

76 Description of registered land

Registered land may be described—

(a) by means of a verbal description and a filed plan or general map, based on the ordnance map; or

(b) by reference to a deed or other document, a copy or extract whereof is filed at the registry, containing a sufficient description, and a plan or map thereof; or

(c) otherwise as the applicant for registration may desire, and the registrar, or, if the applicant prefers, the court, may approve,

regard being had to ready identification of parcels, correct descriptions of boundaries, and, so far as may be, uniformity of practice; but the boundaries of all freehold land and all requisite details in relation to the same, shall whenever practicable, be entered on the register or filed plan, or general map, and the filed plan, if any, or general map shall be used for assisting the identification of the land.

Part VII
Rectification of Register and Indemnity

82 Rectification of the register

(1) The register may be rectified pursuant to an order of the court or by the registrar, subject to an appeal to the court, in any of the following cases, but subject to the provisions of this section:—

(a) Subject to any express provisions of this Act to the contrary, where a court of competent jurisdiction has decided that any person is entitled to any estate right or interest in or to any registered land or charge, and as a consequence of such decision such court is of opinion that a rectification of the register is required, and makes an order to that effect;

(b) Subject to any express provision of this Act to the contrary, where the court, on the application in the presccribed manner of any person who is aggrieved by any entry made in, or by the omission of any entry from, the register, or by any default being made, or unnecessary delay taking place, in the making of any entry in the register, makes an order for the rectification of the register;

(c) In any case and at any time with the consent of all persons interested;

(d) Where the court or the registrar is satisfied that any entry in the register has been obtained by fraud;

(e) Where two or more persons are, by mistake, registered as proprietors of the same registered estate or of the same charge;

(f) Where a mortgagee has been registered as proprietor of the land instead of as proprietor of a charge and a right of redemption is subsisting;

(g) Where a legal estate has been registered in the name of a person who if the land had not been registered would not have been the estate owner; and

(h) In any other case where, by reason of any error or omission in the register, or by reason of any entry made under a mistake, it may be deemed just to rectify the register.

(2) The register may be rectified under this section, notwithstanding that the rectification may affect any estates, rights, charges, or interests acquired or protected by registration, or by any entry on the register, or otherwise.

(3) The register shall not be rectified, except for the purpose of giving effect to an overriding interest [or an order of the court], so as to affect the title of the proprietor who is in possession—

[(a) unless the proprietor has caused or substantially contributed to the error or omission by fraud or lack of proper care; or]

(b) ...

(c) unless for any other reason, in any particular case, it is considered that it would be unjust not to rectify the register against him.

(4) Where a person is in possession of registered land in right of a minor interest, he shall, for the purposes of this section, be deemed to be in possession as agent for the proprietor.

(5) The registrar shall obey the order of any competent court in relation to any registered land on being served with the order or an official copy thereof.

(6) On every rectification of the register the land certificate and any charge certificate which may be affected shall be produced to the registrar unless an order to the contrary is made by him.

Part X
Miscellaneous Provisions

110 Provisions as between vendor and purchaser

On a sale or other disposition of registered land to a purchaser other than a lessee or chargee—

(1) The vendor shall, notwithstanding any stipulation to the contrary, at his own expense furnish the purchaser ..., if required, with a copy of

the subsisting entries in the register and of any filed plans and copies or abstracts of any documents or any part thereof noted on the register so far as they respectively affect the land to be dealt with (except charges or incumbrances registered or protected on the register which are to be discharged or overridden at or prior to completion):

Provided that—

(a) unless the purchase money exceeds one thousand pounds the costs of the copies and abstracts of the said entries plans and documents shall, in the absence of any stipulation to the contrary, be borne by the purchaser requiring the same;

(b) nothing in this section shall give a purchaser a right to a copy or abstract of a settlement filed at the registry:

(2) the vendor shall, subject to any stipulation to the contrary, at his own expense furnish the purchaser with such copies, abstracts and evidence (if any) in respect of any subsisting rights and interests appurtenant to the registered land as to which the register is not conclusive, and of any matters excepted from the effect of registration as the purchaser would have been entitled to if the land had not been registered:

(3) Except as aforesaid, and notwithstanding any stipulation to the contrary, it shall not be necessary for the vendor to furnish the purchaser with any abstract or other written evidence of title, or any copy or abstract of the land certificate, or of any charge certificate:

(4) Where the register refers to a filed abstract or copy of or extract from a deed or other document such abstract or extract shall as between vendor and purchaser be assumed to be correct, and to contain all material portions of the original, and no person dealing with any registered land or charge shall have a right to require production of the original, or be affected in any way by any provisions of the said document other that those appearing in such abstract, copy or extract, and any person suffering loss by reason of any error or omission in such abstract, copy or extract shall be entitled to be indemnified under this Act:

(5) Where the vendor is not himself registered as proprietor of the land or the charge giving a power of sale over the land, he shall, at the request of the puchaser and at his own expense, and notwithstanding any stipulation to the contrary, either procure the registration of himself as proprietor of the land or of the charge, as the case may be, or procure a disposition from the proprietor to the purchaser:

(6) Unless the certificate is deposited at the registry the vendor shall deliver the land certificate, or the charge certificate, as the case may be, to the purchaser on completion of the purchase, or, if only a part of the land comprised in the certificate is dealt with, or only a derivative estate is created, he shall, at his own expense, produce, or procure the production of, the certificate in accordance with this Act for the completion of the purchaser's registration. Where the certificate has been lost or destroyed, the vendor shall, notwithstanding any stipulation to the contrary, pay the costs of the proceedings required to enable the registrar to proceed without it:

(7) The purchaser shall not, by reason of the registration, be affected with notice of any pending action, writ, order, deed of arrangement or land charge (other than a local land charge) to which this subsection applies, which can be protected under this Act by lodging or registering a creditors' notice, restriction, inhibition, caution or other notice, or be concerned to make any search therefor if and so far as they affect registered land.

This subsection applies only to pending actions, writs, orders, deeds of arrangement and land charges (not including local land charges) required to be registered or re-registered after the commencement of this Act, either under the Land Charges Act 1925, or any other statute registration whereunder has effect as if made under that Act.

Land Registration Rules 1925, rule 278

278 General boundaries

(1) Except in cases in which it is noted in the Property Register that the boundaries have been fixed, the filed plan or General Map shall be deemed to indicate the general boundaries only.

(2) In such cases the exact line of the boundary will be left undetermined—as, for instance, whether it includes a hedge or wall and ditch, or runs along the centre of a wall or fence, or its inner or outer face, or how far it runs within or beyond it; or whether or not the land registered includes the whole or any portion of an adjoining road or stream.

(3) When a general boundary only is desired to be entered in the register, notice to the owners of the adjoining lands need not be given.

(4) This rule shall apply notwithstanding that a part or the whole of a ditch, wall, fence, road, stream, or other boundary is expressly included in or excluded from the title or that it forms the whole of the land comprised in the title.

Limitation Act 1980, sections 15, 28 and Schedule 1

Actions to recover land and rent

15 Time limit for actions to recover land

(1) No action shall be brought by any person to recover any land after the expiration of twelve years from the date on which the right of action accrued to him or, if it first accrued to some person through whom he claims, to that person.

(2) Subject to the following provisions of this section, where—

(a) the estate or interest claimed was an estate or interest in reversion or remainder or any other future estate or interest and the right of action to recover the land accrued on the date on which the estate or interest fell into possession by the determination of the preceding estate or interest; and

(b) the person entitled to the preceding estate or interest (not being a term of years absolute) was not in possession of the land on that date;

no action shall be brought by the person entitled to the succeeding estate or interest after the expiration of twelve years from the date on which the right of action accrued to the person entitled to the preceding estate or interest or six years from the date on which the right of action accrued to the person entitled to the succeeding estate or interest, whichever period last expires.

(3) Subsection (2) above shall not apply to any estate or interest which falls into possession on the determination of an entailed interest and which might have been barred by the person entitled to the entailed interest.

(4) No person shall bring an action to recover any estate or interest in land under an assurance taking effect after the right of action to recover the land had accrued to the person by whom the assurance was made or some person through whom he claimed or some person entitled to a preceding estate or interest, unless the action is brought within the period during which the person by whom the assurance was made could have brought such an action.

(5) Where any person is entitled to any estate or interest in land in possession and, while so entitled, is also entitled to any future estate or interest in that land, and his right to recover the estate or interest in possession is barred under this Act, no action shall be brought by that person, or by any person claiming through him, in respect of the future estate or interest, unless in the meantime possession of the land has been recovered by a person entitled to an intermediate estate or interest.

(6) Part I of Schedule 1 to this Act contains provisions for determining the date of accrual of rights of action to recover land in the cases there mentioned.

(7) Part II of that Schedule contains provisions modifying the provisions of this section in their application to actions brought by, or by a person claiming through, the Crown or any spiritual or eleemosynary corporation sole.

Part II
Extension or exclusion of ordinary time limits

Disability

28 Extension of limitation period in case of disability

(1) Subject to the following provisions of this section, if on the date when any right of action accrued for which a period of limitation is prescribed by this Act, the person to whom it accrued was under a disability, the action may be brought at any time before the expiration of six years from the date when he ceased to be under a disability or died (whichever first occurred) notwithstanding that the period of limitation has expired.

(2) This section shall not affect any case where the right of action first accrued to some person (not under a disability) through whom the person under a disability claims.

(3) When a right of action which has accrued to a person under a disability accrues, on the death of that person while still under a disability, to another person under a disability, no further extension of time shall be allowed by reason of the disability of the second person.

(4) No action to recover land or money charged on land shall be brought by virtue of this section by any person after the expiration of thirty years from the date on which the right of action accrued to that person or some person through whom he claims.

[(4A) If the action is one to which section 4A of this Act applies, subsection (1) above shall have effect—

(a) in the case of an action for libel or slander, as if for the words from "at any time" to "occurred)" there were substituted the words "by him at any time before the expiration of one year from the date on which he ceased to be under a disability"; and

(b) in the case of an action for slander of title, slander of goods or other malicious falsehood, as if for the words "six years" there were substituted the words "one year".]

(5)   If the action is one to which section 10 of this Act applies, subsection (1) above shall have effect as if for the words "six years" there were substituted the words "two years".

(6)   If the action is one to which section 11 or 12(2) of this Act applies, subsection (1) above shall have effect as if for the words "six years" there were substituted the words "three years".

[(7) If the action is one to which section 11A of this Act applies or one by virtue of section 6(1)(a) of the Consumer Protection Act 1987 (death caused by defective product), subsection (1) above—

(a) shall not apply to the time limit prescribed by subsection (3) of the said section 11A or to that time limit as applied by virtue of section 12(1) of this Act; and

(b) in relation to any other time limit prescribed by this Act shall have effect as if for the words "six years" there were substituted the words "three years".]

Schedules

Schedule 1

Section 15(6), (7)

Provisions with respect to actions to recover land

Part 1
Accrual of rights of action to recover land

Accrual of right of action in case of present interests in land

1. Where the person bringing an action to recover land, or some person through whom he claims, has been in possession of the land, and has while entitled to the land been dispossessed or discontinued his possession, the right of action shall be treated as having accrued on the date of the dispossession or discontinuance.

2. Where any person brings an action to recover any land of a deceased person (whether under a will or on intestacy) and the deceased person—

    (a) was on the date of his death in possession of the land or, in the case of a rentcharge created by will or taking effect upon his death, in possession of the land charged; and

    (b) was the last person entitled to the land to be in possession of it;

    the right of action shall be treated as having accrued on the date of his death.

3. Where any person brings an action to recover land, being as estate or interest in possession assured otherwise than by will to him, or to some person through whom he claims, and—

    (a) the person making the assurance was on the date when the assurance took effect in possession of the land or, in the case of a rentcharge created by the assurance, in possession of the land charged; and

    (b) no person has been in possession of the land by virtue of the assurance;

    the right of action shall be treated as having accrued on the date when the assurance took effect.

Accrual of right of action in case of future interests

4.   The right of action to recover any land shall, in a case where—

(a) the estate or interest claimed was an estate or interest in reversion or remainder or any other future estate or interest; and

(b) no person has taken possession of the land by virtue of the estate or interest claimed;

be treated as having accrued on the date on which the estate or interest fell into possession by the determination of the preceding estate or interest.

5.— (1) Subject to sub-paragraph (2) below, a tenancy from year to year or other period, without a lease in writing, shall for the purposes of this Act be treated as being determined at the expiration of the first year or other period; and accordingly the right of action of the person entitled to the land subject to the tenancy shall be treated as having accrued at the date on which in accordance with this sub-paragraph the tenancy is determined.

(2) Where any rent has subsequently been received in respect of the tenancy, the right of action shall be treated as having accrued on the date of the last receipt of rent.

6.— (1) Where—

(a) any person is in possession of land by virtue of a lease in writing by which a rent of not less than ten pounds a year is reserved; and

(b) the rent is received by some person wrongfully claiming to be entitled to the land in reversion immediately expectant on the determination of the lease; and

(c) no rent is subsequently received by the person rightfully so entitled;

the right of action to recover the land of the person rightfully so entitled shall be treated as having accrued on the date when the rent was first received by the person wrongfully claiming to be so entitled and not on the date of the determination of the lease.

(2) Sub-paragraph (1) above shall not apply to any lease granted by the Crown.

Accrual of right of action in case of forfeiture or breach of condition

7.— (1) Subject to sub-paragraph (2) below, a right of action to recover land by virtue of a forfeiture or breach of condition shall be treated as having accrued on the date on which the forfeiture was incurred or the condition broken.

(2) If any such right has accrued to a person entitled to an estate or interest in reversion or remainder and the land was not recovered by virtue of that right, the right of action to recover the land shall not be treated as having accrued to that person until his estate or interest fell into possession, as if no such forfeiture or breach of condition had occurred.

Right of action not to accrue or continue unless there is adverse possession

8.— (1) No right of action to recover land shall be treated as accruing unless the land is in the possession of some person in whose favour the period of limitation can run (referred to below in this paragraph as "adverse possession"); and where under the preceding provisions of this Schedule any such right of action is treated as accruing on a certain date and no person is in adverse possession on that date, the right of action shall not be treated as accruing unless and until adverse possession is taken of the land.

(2) Where a right of action to recover land has accrued and after its accrual, before the right is barred, the land ceases to be in adverse possession, the right of action shall no longer be treated as having accrued and no fresh right of action shall be treated as accruing unless and until the land is again taken into adverse possession.

(3) For the purposes of this paragraph—

(a) possession of any land subject to a rentcharge by a person (other than the person entitled to the rentcharge) who does not pay the rent shall be treated as adverse possession of the rentcharge; and

(b) receipt of rent under a lease by a person wrongfully claiming to be entitled to the land in reversion immediately expectant on the determination of the lease shall be treated as adverse possession of the land.

(4) For the purpose of determining whether a person occupying any land is in adverse possession of the land it shall not be assumed by implication of law that his occupation is by permission of the person entitled to the

land merely by virtue of the fact that his occupation is not inconsistent with the latter's present or future enjoyment of the land.

This provision shall not be taken as prejudicing a finding to the effect that a person's occupation of any land is by implied permission of the person entitled to the land in any case where such a finding is justified on the actual facts of the case.

Possession of beneficiary not adverse to others interested in settled land or land held on trust for sale

9.   Where any settled land or any land [subject to a trust of land] is in the possession of a person entitled to a beneficial interest in the land *or in the proceeds of sale* (not being a person solely or absolutely entitled to the land *or the proceeds*), no right of action to recover the land shall be treated for the purposes of this Act as accruing during that possession to any person in whom the land is vested as tenant for life, statutory owner or trustee, or to any other person entitled to a beneficial interest in the land *or the proceeds of sale*.

Part II

Modifications of section 15 where crown or certain corporations sole are involved

10.   Subject to paragraph 11 below, section 15(1) of this Act shall apply to the bringing of an action to recover any land by the Crown or by any spiritual or eleemosynary corporation sole with the substitution for the reference to twelve years of a reference to thirty years.

11.—(1) An action to recover foreshore may be brought by the Crown at any time before the expiration of sixty years from the date mentioned in section 15(1) of this Act.

(2) Where any right of action to recover land which has ceased to be foreshore but remains in the ownership of the Crown accrued when the land was foreshore, the action may be brought at any time before the expiration of—

(a) sixty years from the date of accrual of the right of action; or

(b) thirty years from the date when the land ceased to be foreshore;

whichever period first expires.

(3) In this paragraph "foreshore" means the shore and bed of the sea and of any tidal water, below the line of the medium high tide between the spring tides and the neap tides.

12. Notwithstanding section 15(1) of this Act, where in the case of any action brought by a person other than the Crown or a spiritual or eleemosynary corporation sole the right of action first accrued to the Crown or any such corporation sole through whom the person in question claims, the action may be brought at any time before the expiration of—

(a) the period during which the action could have been brought by the Crown or the corporation sole; or

(b) twelve years from the date on which the right of action accrued to some person other than the Crown or the corporation sole;

whichever period first expires.

13. Section 15(2) of this Act shall apply in any case where the Crown or a spiritual or eleemosynary corporation sole is entitled to the succeeding estate or interest with the substitution—

(a) for the reference to twelve years of a reference to thirty years; and

(b) for the reference to six years of a reference to twelve years.

Supreme Court Act 1981, section 50

50 Power to award damages as well as, or in substitution for, injunction or specific performance

Where the Court of Appeal or the High Court has jurisdiction to entertain an application for an injunction or specific performance, it may award damages in addition to, or in substitution for, an injunction or specific performance.

County Courts Act 1984, section 38

[38 Remedies available in county courts

(1) Subject to what follows, in any proceedings in a county court the court may make any order which could be made by the High Court if the proceedings were in the High Court.

(2) Any order made by a county court may be—

(a) absolute or conditional;

(b) final or interlocutory.

(3) A county court shall not have power—

(a) to order mandamus, certiorari or prohibition; or

(b) to make any order of a prescribed kind.

(4) Regulations under subsection (3)—

(a) may provide for any of their provisions not to apply in such circumstances or descriptions of case as may be specified in the regulations;

(b) may provide for the transfer of the proceedings to the High Court for the purpose of enabling an order of a kind prescribed under subsection (3) to be made;

(c) may make such provision with respect to matters of procedure as the Lord Chancellor considers expedient; and

(d) may make provision amending or repealing any provision made by or under any enactment, so far as may be necessary or expedient in consequence of the regulations.

(5) In this section "prescribed" means prescribed by regulations made by the Lord Chancellor under this section.

(6) The power to make regulations under this section shall be exercised by statutory instrument.

(7) No such statutory instrument shall be made unless a draft of the instrument has been approved by both Houses of Parliament.]

Access to Neighbouring Land Act 1992, sections 1–3

Access to Neighbouring Land Act 1992 (c. 23)

1.— (1) A person—

    (a) who, for the purpose of carrying out works to any land (the "dominant land"), desires to enter upon any adjoining or adjacent land (the "servient land"), and

    (b) who needs, but does not have, the consent of some other person to that entry,

    may make an application to the court for an order under this section ("an access order") against that other person.

(2) On an application under this section, the court shall make an access order if, and only if, it is satisfied—

    (a) that the works are reasonably necessary for the preservation of the whole or any part of the dominant land; and

    (b) that they cannot be carried out, or would be substantially more difficult to carry out, without entry upon the servient land;

    but this subsection is subject to subsection (3) below.

(3) The court shall not make an access order in any case where it is satisfied that, were it to make such an order—

    (a) the respondent or any other person would suffer interference with, or disturbance of, his use or enjoyment of the servient land, or

    (b) the respondent, or any other person (whether of full age or capacity or not) in occupation of the whole or any part of the servient land, would suffer hardship,

    to such a degree by reason of the entry (notwithstanding any requirement of this Act or any term or condition that may be imposed under it) that it would be unreasonable to make the order.

(4) Where the court is satisfied on an application under this section that it is reasonably necessary to carry out any basic preservation works to the dominant land, those works shall be taken for the purposes of this Act to be reasonably necessary for the preservation of the land;

and in this subsection "basic preservation works" means any of the following, that is to say—

(a) the maintenance, repair or renewal of any part of a building or other structure comprised in, or situate on, the dominant land;

(b) the clearance, repair or renewal of any drain, sewer, pipe or cable so comprised or situate;

(c) the treatment, cutting back, felling, removal or replacement of any hedge, tree, shrub or other growing thing which is so comprised and which is, or is in danger of becoming, damaged, diseased, dangerous, insecurely rooted or dead;

(d) the filling in, or clearance, of any ditch so comprised;

but this subsection is without prejudice to the generality of the works which may, apart from it, be regarded by the court as reasonably necessary for the preservation of any land.

(5) If the court considers it fair and reasonable in all the circumstances of the case, works may be regarded for the purposes of this Act as being reasonably necessary for the preservation of any land (or, for the purposes of subsection (4) above, as being basic preservation works which it is reasonably necessary to carry out to any land) notwithstanding that the works incidentally involve—

(a) the making of some alteration, adjustment or improvement to the land, or

(b) the demolition of the whole or any part of a building or structure comprised in or situate upon the land.

(6) Where any works are reasonably necessary for the preservation of the whole or any part of the dominant land, the doing to the dominant land of anything which is requisite for, incidental to, or consequential on, the carrying out of those works shall be treated for the purposes of this Act as the carrying out of works which are reasonably necessary for the preservation of that land; and references in this Act to works, or to the carrying out of works, shall be construed accordingly.

(7) Without prejudice to the generality of subsection (6) above, if it is reasonably necessary for a person to inspect the dominant land—

(a) for the purpose of ascertaining whether any works may be reasonably necessary for the preservation of the whole or any part of that land,

(b) for the purpose of making any map or plan, or ascertaining the course of any drain, sewer, pipe or cable, in preparation for, or otherwise in connection with, the carrying out of works which are so reasonably necessary, or

(c) otherwise in connection with the carrying out of any such works,

the making of such an inspection shall be taken for the purposes of this Act to be the carrying out to the dominant land of works which are reasonably necessary for the preservation of that land; and references in this Act to works, or to the carrying out of works, shall be construed accordingly.

2.— (1) An access order shall specify—

(a) the works to the dominant land that may be carried out by entering upon the servient land in pursuance of the order;

(b) the particular area of servient land that may be entered upon by virtue of the order for the purpose of carrying out those works to the dominant land; and

(c) the date on which, or the period during which, the land may be so entered upon;

and in the following provisions of this Act any reference to the servient land is a reference to the area specified in the order in pursuance of paragraph (b) above.

(2) An access order may impose upon the applicant or the respondent such terms and conditions as appear to the court to be reasonably necessary for the purpose of avoiding or restricting—

(a) any loss, damage, or injury which might otherwise be caused to the respondent or any other person by reason of the entry authorised by the order; or

(b) any inconvenience or loss of privacy that might otherwise be so caused to the respondent or any other person.

(3) Without prejudice to the generality of subsection (2) above, the terms and conditions which may be imposed under that subsection include provisions with respect to—

(a) the manner in which the specified works are to be carried out;

(b) the days on which, and the hours between which, the work involved may be executed;

(c) the persons who may undertake the carrying out of the specified works or enter upon the servient land under or by virtue of the order;

(d) the taking of any such precautions by the applicant as may be specified in the order.

(4) An access order may also impose terms and conditions—

(a) requiring the applicant to pay, or to secure that such person connected with him as may be specified in the order pays, compensation for—

(i) any loss, damage or injury, or

(ii) any substantial loss of privacy or other substantial inconvenience,

which will, or might, be caused to the respondent or any other person by reason of the entry authorised by the order;

(b) requiring the applicant to secure that he, or such person connected with him as may be specified in the order, is insured against any such risks as may be so specified; or

(c) requiring such a record to be made of the condition of the servient land, or of such part of it as may be so specified, as the court may consider expedient with a view to facilitating the determination of any question that may arise concerning damage to that land.

(5) An access order may include provision requiring the applicant to pay the respondent such sum by way of consideration for the privilege of entering the servient land in pursuance of the order as appears to the court to be fair and reasonable having regard to all the circumstances of the case, including, in particular—

(a) the likely financial advantage of the order to the applicant and any persons connected with him; and

(b) the degree of inconvenience likely to be caused to the respondent or any other person by the entry;

but no payment shall be ordered under this subsection if and to the extent that the works which the applicant desires to carry out by means of the entry are works to residential land.

(6) For the purposes of subsection (5)(a) above, the likely financial advantage of an access order to the applicant and any persons

connected with him shall in all cases be taken to be a sum of money equal to the greater of the following amounts, that is to say—

(a) the amount (if any) by which so much of any likely increase in the value of any land—

    (i) which consists of or includes the dominant land, and

    (ii) which is owned or occupied by the same person as the dominant land,

as may reasonably be regarded as attributable to the carrying out of the specified works exceeds the likely cost of carrying out those works with the benefit of the access order; and

(b) the difference (if it would have been possible to carry out the specified works without entering upon the servient land) between—

    (i) the likely cost of carrying out those works without entering upon the servient land; and

    (ii) the likely cost of carrying them out with the benefit of the access order.

(7) For the purposes of subsection (5) above, "residential land" means so much of any land as consists of—

(a) a dwelling or part of a dwelling;

(b) a garden, yard, private garage or outbuilding which is used and enjoyed wholly or mainly with a dwelling; or

(c) in the case of a building which includes one or more dwellings, any part of the building which is used and enjoyed wholly or mainly with those dwellings or any of them.

(8) The persons who are to be regarded for the purposes of this section as "connected with" the applicant are—

(a) the owner of any estate or interest in, or right over, the whole or any part of the dominant land;

(b) the occupier of the whole or any part of the dominant land; and

(c) any person whom the applicant may authorise under section 3(7) below to exercise the power of entry conferred by the access order.

(9) The court may make provision—

(a) for the reimbursement by the applicant of any expenses reasonably incurred by the respondent in connection with the application which are not otherwise recoverable as costs;

(b) for the giving of security by the applicant for any sum that might become payable to the respondent or any other person by virtue of this section or section 3 below.

3.— (1) An access order requires the respondent, so far as he has power to do so, to permit the applicant or any of his associates to do anything which the applicant or associate is authorised or required to do under or by virtue of the order or this section.

(2) Except as otherwise provided by or under this Act, an access order authorises the applicant or any of his associates, without the consent of the respondent,—

(a) to enter upon the servient land for the purpose of carrying out the specified works;

(b) to bring on to that land, leave there during the period permitted by the order and, before the end of that period, remove, such materials, plant and equipment as are reasonably necessary for the carrying out of those works; and

(c) to bring on to that land any waste arising from the carrying out of those works, if it is reasonably necessary to do so in the course of removing it from the dominant land;

but nothing in this Act or in any access order shall authorise the applicant or any of his associates to leave anything in, on or over the servient land (otherwise than in discharge of their duty to make good that land) after their entry for the purpose of carrying out works to the dominant land ceases to be authorised under or by virtue of the order.

(3) An access order requires the applicant—

(a) to secure that any waste arising from the carrying out of the specified works is removed from the servient land forthwith;

(b) to secure that, before the entry ceases to be authorised under or by virtue of the order, the servient land is, so far as reasonably practicable, made good; and

(c) to indemnify the respondent against any damage which may be caused to the servient land or any goods by the applicant or any of his associates which would not have been so caused had the order not been made;

but this subsection is subject to subsections (4) and (5) below.

(4) In making an access order, the court may vary or exclude, in whole or in part,—

(a) any authorisation that would otherwise be conferred by subsection (2)(b) or (c) above; or

(b) any requirement that would otherwise be imposed by subsection (3) above.

(5) Without prejudice to the generality of subsection (4) above, if the court is satisfied that it is reasonably necessary for any such waste as may arise from the carrying out of the specified works to be left on the servient land for some period before removal, the access order may, in place of subsection (3)(a) above, include provision—

(a) authorising the waste to be left on that land for such period as may be permitted by the order; and

(b) requiring the applicant to secure that the waste is removed before the end of that period.

(6) Where the applicant or any of his associates is authorised or required under or by virtue of an access order or this section to enter, or do any other thing, upon the servient land, he shall not (as respects that access order) be taken to be a trespasser from the beginning on account of his, or any other person's, subsequent conduct.

(7) For the purposes of this section, the applicant's "associates" are such number of persons (whether or not servants or agents of his) whom he may reasonably authorise under this subsection to exercise the power of entry conferred by the access order as may be reasonably necessary for carrying out the specified works.

Party Wall etc. Act 1996 (c.40)

Construction and repair of walls on line of junction

1.— (1) This section shall have effect where lands of different owners adjoin and–

(a) are not built on at the line of junction; or

(b) are built on at the line of junction only to the extent of a boundary wall (not being a party fence wall or the external wall of a building),

and either owner is about to build on any part of the line of junction.

(2) If a building owner desires to build a party wall or party fence wall on the line of junction he shall, at least one month before he intends the building work to start, serve on any adjoining owner a notice which indicates his desire to build and describes the intended wall.

(3) If, having been served with notice described in subsection (2), an adjoining owner serves on the building owner a notice indicating his consent to the building of a party wall or party fence wall–

(a) the wall shall be built half on the land of each of the two owners or in such other position as may be agreed between the two owners; and

(b) the expense of building the wall shall be from time to time defrayed by the two owners in such proportion as has regard to the use made or to be made of the wall by each of them and to the cost of labour and materials prevailing at the time when that use is made by each owner respectively.

(4) If, having been served with notice described in subsection (2), an adjoining owner does not consent under this subsection to the building of a party wall or party fence wall, the building owner may only build the wall–

(a) at his own expense; and

(b) as an external wall or a fence wall, as the case may be, placed wholly on his own land,

and consent under this subsection is consent by a notice served within the period of fourteen days beginning with the day on which the notice described in subsection (2) is served.

(5) If the building owner desires to build on the line of junction a wall placed wholly on his own land he shall, at least one month before he intends the building work to start, serve on any adjoining owner a notice which indicates his desire to build and describes the intended wall.

(6) Where the building owner builds a wall wholly on his own land in accordance with subsection (4) or (5) he shall have the right, at any time in the period which–

(a) begins one month after the day on which the notice mentioned in the subsection concerned was served, and

(b) ends twelve months after that day,

to place below the level of the land of the adjoining owner such projecting footings and foundations as are necessary for the construction of the wall.

(7) Where the building owner builds a wall wholly on his own land in accordance with subsection (4) or (5) he shall do so at his own expense and shall compensate any adjoining owner and any adjoining occupier for any damage to his property occasioned by–

(a) the building of the wall;

(b) the placing of any footings or foundations placed in accordance with subsection (6).

(8) Where any dispute arises under this section between the building owner and any adjoining owner or occupier it is to be determined in accordance with section 10.

2.— (1) This section applies where lands of different owners adjoin and at the line of junction the said lands are built on or a boundary wall, being a party fence wall or the external wall of a building, has been erected.

(2) A building owner shall have the following rights–

(a) to underpin, thicken or raise a party structure, a party fence wall, or an external wall which belongs to the building owner and is built against a party structure or party fence wall;

(b) to make good, repair, or demolish and rebuild, a party structure or party fence wall in a case where such work is necessary on account of defect or want of repair of the structure or wall;

(c) to demolish a partition which separates buildings belonging to different owners but does not conform with statutory requirements and to build instead a party wall which does so conform;

(d) in the case of buildings connected by arches or structures over public ways or over passages belonging to other persons, to demolish the whole or part of such buildings, arches or structures which do not conform with statutory requirements and to rebuild them so that they do so conform;

(e) to demolish a party structure which is of insufficient strength or height for the purposes of any intended building of the building owner and to rebuild it of sufficient strength or height for the said purposes (including rebuilding to a lesser height or thickness where the rebuilt structure is of sufficient strength and height for the purposes of any adjoining owner);

(f) to cut into a party structure for any purpose (which may be or include the purpose of inserting a damp proof course);

(g) to cut away from a party wall, party fence wall, external wall or boundary wall any footing or any projecting chimney breast, jamb or flue, or other projection on or over the land of the building owner in order to erect, raise or underpin any such wall or for any other purpose;

(h) to cut away or demolish parts of any wall or building of an adjoining owner overhanging the land of the building owner or overhanging a party wall, to the extent that it is necessary to cut away or demolish the parts to enable a vertical wall to be erected or raised against the wall or building of the adjoining owner;

(j) to cut into the wall of an adjoining owner's building in order to insert a flashing or other weather-proofing of a wall erected against that wall;

(k) to execute any other necessary works incidental to the connection of a party structure with the premises adjoining it;

(l) to raise a party fence wall, or to raise such a wall for use as a party wall, and to demolish a party fence wall and rebuild it as a party fence wall or as a party wall;

(m) subject to the provisions of section 11(7), to reduce, or to demolish and rebuild, a party wall or party fence wall to–

  (i) a height of not less than two metres where the wall is not used by an adjoining owner to any greater extent than a boundary wall; or

  (ii) a height currently enclosed upon by the building of an adjoining owner;

(n) to expose a party wall or party structure hitherto enclosed subject to providing adequate weathering.

(3) Where work mentioned in paragraph (a) of subsection (2) is not necessary on account of defect or want of repair of the structure or wall concerned, the right falling within that paragraph is exercisable–

(a) subject to making good all damage occasioned by the work to the adjoining premises or to their internal furnishings and decorations; and

(b) where the work is to a party structure or external wall, subject to carrying any relevant flues and chimney stacks up to such a height and in such materials as may be agreed between the building owner and the adjoining owner concerned or, in the event of dispute, determined in accordance with section 10;

and relevant flues and chimney stacks are those which belong to an adjoining owner and either form part of or rest on or against the party structure or external wall.

(4) The right falling within subsection (2)(e) is exercisable subject to–

(a) making good all damage occasioned by the work to the adjoining premises or to their internal furnishings and decorations; and

(b) carrying any relevant flues and chimney stacks up to such a height and in such materials as may be agreed between the building owner and the adjoining owner concerned or, in the event of dispute, determined in accordance with section 10;

and relevant flues and chimney stacks are those which belong to an adjoining owner and either form part of or rest on or against the party structure.

(5) Any right falling within subsection (2)(f), (g) or (h) is exercisable subject to making good all damage occasioned by the work to the adjoining premises or to their internal furnishings and decorations.

(6) The right falling within subsection (2)(j) is exercisable subject to making good all damage occasioned by the work to the wall of the adjoining owner's building.

(7) The right falling within subsection (2)(m) is exercisable subject to–

(a) reconstructing any parapet or replacing an existing parapet with another one; or

(b) constructing a parapet where one is needed but did not exist before.

(8) For the purposes of this section a building or structure which was erected before the day on which this Act was passed shall be deemed to conform with statutory requirements if it conforms with the statutes regulating buildings or structures on the date on which it was erected.

3.— (1) Before exercising any right conferred on him by section 2 a building owner shall serve on any adjoining owner a notice (in this Act referred to as a "party structure notice") stating–

(a) the name and address of the building owner;

(b) the nature and particulars of the proposed work including, in cases where the building owner proposes to construct special foundations, plans, sections and details of construction of the special foundations together with reasonable particulars of the loads to be carried thereby; and

(c) the date on which the proposed work will begin.

(2) A party structure notice shall–

(a) be served at least two months before the date on which the proposed work will begin;

(b) cease to have effect if the work to which it relates–

(i) has not begun within the period of twelve months beginning with the day on which the notice is served; and

(ii) is not prosecuted with due diligence.

(3) Nothing in this section shall–

(a) prevent a building owner from exercising with the consent in writing of the adjoining owners and of the adjoining occupiers any right conferred on him by section 2; or

(b) require a building owner to serve any party structure notice before complying with any notice served under any statutory provisions relating to dangerous or neglected structures.

4.— (1) An adjoining owner may, having been served with a party structure notice serve on the building owner a notice (in this Act referred to as a "counter notice") setting out–

(a) in respect of a party fence wall or party structure, a requirement that the building owner build in or on the wall or structure to which the notice relates such chimney copings, breasts, jambs or flues, or such piers or recesses or other like works, as may reasonably be required for the convenience of the adjoining owner;

(b) in respect of special foundations to which the adjoining owner consents under section 7(4) below, a requirement that the special foundations–

(i) be placed at a specified greater depth than that proposed by the building owner; or

(ii) be constructed of sufficient strength to bear the load to be carried by columns of any intended building of the adjoining owner,

or both.

(2) A counter notice shall–

(a) specify the works required by the notice to be executed and shall be accompanied by plans, sections and particulars of such works; and

(b) be served within the period of one month beginning with the day on which the party structure notice is served.

(3) A building owner on whom a counter notice has been served shall comply with the requirements of the counter notice unless the execution of the works required by the counter notice would–

(a) be injurious to him;

(b) cause unnecessary inconvenience to him; or

(c) cause unnecessary delay in the execution of the works pursuant to the party structure notice.

5.   If an owner on whom a party structure notice or a counter notice has been served does not serve a notice indicating his consent to it within the

period of fourteen days beginning with the day on which the party structure notice or counter notice was served, he shall be deemed to have dissented from the notice and a dispute shall be deemed to have arisen between the parties.

Adjacent excavation and construction

6.— (1)   This section applies where–

(a) a building owner proposes to excavate, or excavate for and erect a building or structure, within a distance of three metres measured horizontally from any part of a building or structure of an adjoining owner; and

(b) any part of the proposed excavation, building or structure will within those three metres extend to a lower level than the level of the bottom of the foundations of the building or structure of the adjoining owne.

(2)   This section also applies where–

(a) a building owner proposes to excavate, or excavate for and erect a building or structure, within a distance of six metres measured horizontally from any part of a building or structure of an adjoining owner; and

(b) any part of the proposed excavation, building or structure will within those six metres meet a plane drawn downwards in the direction of the excavation, building or structure of the building owner at an angle of forty-five degrees to the horizontal from the line formed by the intersection of the plane of the level of the bottom of the foundations of the building or structure of the adjoining owner with the plane of the external face of the external wall of the building or structure of the adjoining owner.

(3)   The building owner may, and if required by the adjoining owner shall, at his own expense underpin or otherwise strengthen or safeguard the foundations of the building or structure of the adjoining owner so far as may be necessary.

(4)   Where the buildings or structures of different owners are within the respective distances mentioned in subsections (1) and (2) the owners of those buildings or structures shall be deemed to be adjoining owners for the purposes of this section.

(5) In any case where this section applies the building owner shall, at least one month before beginning to excavate, or excavate for and erect a building or structure, serve on the adjoining owner a notice indicating his proposals and stating whether he proposes to underpin or otherwise strengthen or safeguard the foundations of the building or structure of the adjoining owner.

(6) The notice referred to in subsection (5) shall be accompanied by plans and sections showing–

(a) the site and depth of any excavation the building owner proposes to make;

(b) if he proposes to erect a building or structure, its site.

(7) If an owner on whom a notice referred to in subsection (5) has been served does not serve a notice indicating his consent to it within the period of fourteen days beginning with the day on which the notice referred to in subsection (5) was served, he shall be deemed to have dissented from the notice and a dispute shall be deemed to have arisen between the parties.

(8) The notice referred to in subsection (5) shall cease to have effect if the work to which the notice relates–

(a) has not begun within the period of twelve months beginning with the day on which the notice was served; and

(b) is not prosecuted with due diligence.

(9) On completion of any work executed in pursuance of this section the building owner shall if so requested by the adjoining owner supply him with particulars including plans and sections of the work.

(10) Nothing in this section shall relieve the building owner from any liability to which he would otherwise be subject for injury to any adjoining owner or any adjoining occupier by reason of work executed by him.

Rights etc.

7.— (1) A building owner shall not exercise any right conferred on him by this Act in such a manner or at such time as to cause unnecessary inconvenience to any adjoining owner or to any adjoining occupier.

(2) The building owner shall compensate any adjoining owner and any adjoining occupier for any loss or damage which may result to any of them by reason of any work executed in pursuance of this Act.

(3) Where a building owner in exercising any right conferred on him by this Act lays open any part of the adjoining land or building he shall at his own expense make and maintain so long as may be necessary a proper hoarding, shoring or fans or temporary construction for the protection of the adjoining land or building and the security of any adjoining occupier.

(4) Nothing in this Act shall authorise the building owner to place special foundations on land of an adjoining owner without his previous consent in writing.

(5) Any works executed in pursuance of this Act shall–

(a) comply with the provisions of statutory requirements; and

(b) be executed in accordance with such plans, sections and particulars as may be agreed between the owners or in the event of dispute determined in accordance with section 10;

and no deviation shall be made from those plans, sections and particulars except such as may be agreed between the owners (or surveyors acting on their behalf) or in the event of dispute determined in accordance with section 10.

8.— (1) A building owner, his servants, agents and workmen may during usual working hours enter and remain on any land or premises for the purpose of executing any work in pursuance of this Act and may remove any furniture or fittings or take any other action necessary for that purpose.

(2) If the premises are closed, the building owner, his agents and workmen may, if accompanied by a constable or other police officer, break open any fences or doors in order to enter the premises.

(3) No land or premises may be entered by any person under subsection (1) unless the building owner serves on the owner and the occupier of the land or premises–

(a) in case of emergency, such notice of the intention to enter as may be reasonably practicable;

(b) in any other case, such notice of the intention to enter as complies with subsection (4).

(4) Notice complies with this subsection if it is served in a period of not less than fourteen days ending with the day of the proposed entry.

(5) A surveyor appointed or selected under section 10 may during usual working hours enter and remain on any land or premises for the purpose of carrying out the object for which he is appointed or selected.

(6) No land or premises may be entered by a surveyor under subsection (5) unless the building owner who is a party to the dispute concerned serves on the owner and the occupier of the land or premises–

> (a) in case of emergency, such notice of the intention to enter as may be reasonably practicable;

> (b) in any other case, such notice of the intention to enter as complies with subsection (4).

9. Nothing in this Act shall–

> (a) authorise any interference with an easement of light or other easements in or relating to a party wall; or

> (b) prejudicially affect any right of any person to preserve or restore any right or other thing in or connected with a party wall in case of the party wall being pulled down or rebuilt.

Resolution of disputes

10.—(1) Where a dispute arises or is deemed to have arisen between a building owner and an adjoining owner in respect of any matter connected with any work to which this Act relates either–

> (a) both parties shall concur in the appointment of one surveyor (in this section referred to as an "agreed surveyor"); or

> (b) each party shall appoint a surveyor and the two surveyors so appointed shall forthwith select a third surveyor (all of whom are in this section referred to as "the three surveyors").

(2) All appointments and selections made under this section shall be in writing and shall not be rescinded by either party.

(3) If an agreed surveyor–

> (a) refuses to act;

> (b) neglects to act for a period of ten days beginning with the day on which either party serves a request on him;

(c) dies before the dispute is settled; or

(d) becomes or deems himself incapable of acting,

the proceedings for settling such dispute shall begin *de novo*.

(4)   If either party to the dispute–

(a) refuses to appoint a surveyor under subsection (1)(b), or

(b) neglects to appoint a surveyor under subsection (1)(b) for a period of ten days beginning with the day on which the other party serves a request on him,

the other party may make the appointment on his behalf.

(5)   If, before the dispute is settled, a surveyor appointed under paragraph (b) of subsection (1) by a party to the dispute dies, or becomes or deems himself incapable of acting, the party who appointed him may appoint another surveyor in his place with the same power and authority.

(6)   If a surveyor–

(a) appointed under paragraph (b) of subsection (1) by a party to the dispute; or

(b) appointed under subsection (4) or (5),

refuses to act effectively, the surveyor of the other party may proceed to act *ex parte* and anything so done by him shall be as effectual as if he had been an agreed surveyor.

(7)   If a surveyor–

(a) appointed under paragraph (b) of subsection (1) by a party to the dispute; or

(b) appointed under subsection (4) or (5),

neglects to act effectively for a period of ten days beginning with the day on which either party or the surveyor of the other party serves a request on him, the surveyor of the other party may proceed to act *ex parte* in respect of the subject matter of the request and anything so done by him shall be as effectual as if he had been an agreed surveyor.

(8)   If either surveyor appointed under subsection (1)(b) by a party to the dispute refuses to select a third surveyor under subsection (1) or

(9), or neglects to do so for a period of ten days beginning with the day on which the other surveyor serves a request on him–

(a) the appointing officer; or

(b) in cases where the relevant appointing officer or his employer is a party to the dispute, the Secretary of State,

may on the application of either surveyor select a third surveyor who shall have the same power and authority as if he had been selected under subsection (1) or subsection (9).

(9) If a third surveyor selected under subsection (1)(b)–

(a) refuses to act;

(b) neglects to act for a period of ten days beginning with the day on which either party or the surveyor appointed by either party serves a request on him; or

(c) dies, or becomes or deems himself incapable of acting, before the dispute is settled,

the other two of the three surveyors shall forthwith select another surveyor in his place with the same power and authority.

(10) The agreed surveyor or as the case may be the three surveyors or any two of them shall settle by award any matter–

(a) which is connected with any work to which this Act relates, and

(b) which is in dispute between the building owner and the adjoining owner.

(11) Either of the parties or either of the surveyors appointed by the parties may call upon the third surveyor selected in pursuance of this section to determine the disputed matters and he shall make the necessary award.

(12) An award may determine–

(a) the right to execute any work;

(b) the time and manner of executing any work; and

(c) any other matter arising out of or incidental to the dispute including the costs of making the award;

but any period appointed by the award for executing any work shall not unless otherwise agreed between the building owner and the adjoining owner begin to run until after the expiration of the period prescribed by this Act for service of the notice in respect of which the dispute arises or is deemed to have arisen.

(13) The reasonable costs incurred in–

(a) making or obtaining an award under this section;

(b) reasonable inspections of work to which the award relates; and

(c) any other matter arising out of the dispute,

shall be paid by such of the parties as the surveyor or surveyors making the award determine.

(14) Where the surveyors appointed by the parties make an award the surveyors shall serve it forthwith on the parties.

(15) Where an award is made by the third surveyor–

(a) he shall, after payment of the costs of the award, serve it forthwith on the parties or their appointed surveyors; and

(b) if it is served on their appointed surveyors, they shall serve it forthwith on the parties.

(16) The award shall be conclusive and shall not except as provided by this section be questioned in any court.

(17) Either of the parties to the dispute may, within the period of fourteen days beginning with the day on which an award made under this section is served on him, appeal to the county court against the award and the county court may–

(a) rescind the award or modify it in such manner as the court thinks fit; and

(b) make such order as to costs as the court thinks fit.

Expenses

11.—(1) Except as provided under this section expenses of work under this Act shall be defrayed by the building owner.

(2) Any dispute as to responsibility for expenses shall be settled as provided in section 10.

(3) An expense mentioned in section 1(3)(b) shall be defrayed as there mentioned.

(4) Where work is carried out in exercise of the right mentioned in section 2(2)(a), and the work is necessary on account of defect or want of repair of the structure or wall concerned, the expenses shall be defrayed by the building owner and the adjoining owner in such proportion as has regard to—

    (a) the use which the owners respectively make or may make of the structure or wall concerned; and

    (b) responsibility for the defect or want of repair concerned, if more than one owner makes use of the structure or wall concerned.

(5) Where work is carried out in exercise of the right mentioned in section 2(2)(b) the expenses shall be defrayed by the building owner and the adjoining owner in such proportion as has regard to—

    (a) the use which the owners respectively make or may make of the structure or wall concerned; and

    (b) responsibility for the defect or want of repair concerned, if more than one owner makes use of the structure or wall concerned.

(6) Where the adjoining premises are laid open in exercise of the right mentioned in section 2(2)(e) a fair allowance in respect of disturbance and inconvenience shall be paid by the building owner to the adjoining owner or occupier.

(7) Where a building owner proposes to reduce the height of a party wall or party fence wall under section 2(2)(m) the adjoining owner may serve a counter notice under section 4 requiring the building owner to maintain the existing height of the wall, and in such case the adjoining owner shall pay to the building owner a due proportion of the cost of the wall so far as it exceeds—

    (a) two metres in height; or

    (b) the height currently enclosed upon by the building of the adjoining owner.

(8) Where the building owner is required to make good damage under this Act the adjoining owner has a right to require that the expenses of such making good be determined in accordance with section 10 and paid to him in lieu of the carrying out of work to make the damage good.

(9) Where–

    (a) works are carried out, and

    (b) some of the works are carried out at the request of the adjoining owner or in pursuance of a requirement made by him,

he shall defray the expenses of carrying out the works requested or required by him.

(10) Where–

    (a) consent in writing has been given to the construction of special foundations on land of an adjoining owner; and

    (b) the adjoining owner erects any building or structure and its cost is found to be increased by reason of the existence of the said foundations,

the owner of the building to which the said foundations belong shall, on receiving an account with any necessary invoices and other supporting documents within the period of two months beginning with the day of the completion of the work by the adjoining owner, repay to the adjoining owner so much of the cost as is due to the existence of the said foundations.

(11) Where use is subsequently made by the adjoining owner of work carried out solely at the expense of the building owner the adjoining owner shall pay a due proportion of the expenses incurred by the building owner in carrying out that work; and for this purpose he shall be taken to have incurred expenses calculated by reference to what the cost of the work would be if it were carried out at the time when that subsequent use is made.

12.—(1) An adjoining owner may serve a notice requiring the building owner before he begins any work in the exercise of the rights conferred by this Act to give such security as may be agreed between the owners or in the event of dispute determined in accordance with section 10.

    (2) Where–

    (a) in the exercise of the rights conferred by this Act an adjoining owner requires the building owner to carry out any work the expenses of which are to be defrayed in whole or in part by the adjoining owner; or

    (b) an adjoining owner serves a notice on the building owner under subsection (1), the building owner may before beginning the work to which the requirement or notice relates serve a notice on the adjoining owner requiring him to give such security as may be agreed between the owners or in the event of dispute determined in accordance with section 10.

(3) If within the period of one month beginning with–

(a) the day on which a notice is served under subsection (2); or

(b) in the event of dispute, the date of the determination by the surveyor or surveyors,

the adjoining owner does not comply with the notice or the determination, the requirement or notice by him to which the building owner's notice under that subsection relates shall cease to have effect.

13.—(1) Within the period of two months beginning with the day of the completion of any work executed by a building owner of which the expenses are to be wholly or partially defrayed by an adjoining owner in accordance with section 11 the building owner shall serve on the adjoining owner an account in writing showing–

(a) particulars and expenses of the work; and

(b) any deductions to which the adjoining owner or any other person is entitled in respect of old materials or otherwise;

and in preparing the account the work shall be estimated and valued at fair average rates and prices according to the nature of the work, the locality and the cost of labour and materials prevailing at the time when the work is executed.

(2) Within the period of one month beginning with the day of service of the said account the adjoining owner may serve on the building owner a notice stating any objection he may have thereto and thereupon a dispute shall be deemed to have arisen between the parties.

(3) If within that period of one month the adjoining owner does not serve notice under subsection (2) he shall be deemed to have no objection to the account.

14.—(1)   All expenses to be defrayed by an adjoining owner in accordance with an account served under section 13 shall be paid by the adjoining owner.

(2)   Until an adjoining owner pays to the building owner such expenses as aforesaid the property in any works executed under this Act to which the expenses relate shall be vested solely in the building owner.

Miscellaneous

15.—(1)   A notice or other document required or authorised to be served under this Act may be served on a person–

(a) by delivering it to him in person;

(b) by sending it by post to him at his usual or last-known residence or place of business in the United Kingdom; or

(c) in the case of a body corporate, by delivering it to the secretary or clerk of the body corporate at its registered or principal office or sending it by post to the secretary or clerk of that body corporate at that office.

(2) In the case of a notice or other document required or authorised to be served under this Act on a person as owner of premises, it may alternatively be served by–

(a) addressing it "the owner" of the premises (naming them), and

(b) delivering it to a person on the premises or, if no person to whom it can be delivered is found there, fixing it to a conspicuous part of the premises.

16.—(1) If–

(a) an occupier of land or premises refuses to permit a person to do anything which he is entitled to do with regard to the land or premises under section 8(1) or (5); and

(b) the occupier knows or has reasonable cause to believe that the person is so entitled,

the occupier is guilty of an offence.

(2) If–

   (a) a person hinders or obstructs a person in attempting to do anything which he is entitled to do with regard to land or premises under section 8(1) or (5); and

   (b) the first-mentioned person knows or has reasonable cause to believe that the other person is so entitled,

   the first-mentioned person is guilty of an offence.

(3) A person guilty of an offence under subsection (1) or (2) is liable on summary conviction to a fine of an amount not exceeding level 3 on the standard scale.

17. Any sum payable in pursuance of this Act (otherwise than by way of fine) shall be recoverable summarily as a civil debt.

18.— (1) This Act shall not apply to land which is situated in inner London and in which there is an interest belonging to–

   (a) the Honourable Society of the Inner Temple,

   (b) the Honourable Society of the Middle Temple,

   (c) the Honourable Society of Lincoln's Inn, or

   (d) the Honourable Society of Gray's Inn.

(2) The reference in subsection (1) to inner London is to Greater London other than the outer London boroughs.

19.— (1) This Act shall apply to land in which there is–

   (a) an interest belonging to Her Majesty in right of the Crown,

   (b) an interest belonging to a government department, or

   (c) an interest held in trust for Her Majesty for the purposes of any such department.

(2) This Act shall apply to–

   (a) land which is vested in, but not occupied by, Her Majesty in right of the Duchy of Lancaster;

   (b) land which is vested in, but not occupied by, the possessor for the time being of the Duchy of Cornwall.

20. In this Act, unless the context otherwise requires, the following expressions have the meanings hereby respectively assigned to them–

"adjoining owner" and "adjoining occupier" respectively mean any owner and any occupier of land, buildings, storeys or rooms adjoining those of the building owner and for the purposes only of section 6 within the distances specified in that section;

"appointing officer" means the person appointed under this Act by the local authority to make such appointments as are required under section 10(8);

"building owner" means an owner of land who is desirous of exercising rights under this Act;

"foundation", in relation to a wall, means the solid ground or artificially formed support resting on solid ground on which the wall rests;

"owner" includes–

(a) a person in receipt of, or entitled to receive, the whole or part of the rents or profits of land;

(b) a person in possession of land, otherwise than as a mortgagee or as a tenant from year to year or for a lesser term or as a tenant at will;

(c) a purchaser of an interest in land under a contract for purchase or under an agreement for a lease, otherwise than under an agreement for a tenancy from year to year or for a lesser term;

"party fence wall" means a wall (not being part of a building) which stands on lands of different owners and is used or constructed to be used for separating such adjoining lands, but does not include a wall constructed on the land of one owner the artificially formed support of which projects into the land of another owner;

"party structure" means a party wall and also a floor partition or other structure separating buildings or parts of buildings approached solely by separate staircases or separate entrances;

"party wall" means–

(a) a wall which forms part of a building and stands on lands of different owners to a greater extent than the projection of any artificially formed support on which the wall rests; and

(b) so much of a wall not being a wall referred to in paragraph (a) above as separates buildings belonging to different owners;

"special foundations" means foundations in which an assemblage of beams or rods is employed for the purpose of distributing any load; and

"surveyor" means any person not being a party to the matter appointed or selected under section 10 to determine disputes in accordance with the procedures set out in this Act.

21.—(1) The Secretary of State may by order amend or repeal any provision of a private or local Act passed before or in the same session as this Act, if it appears to him necessary or expedient to do so in consequence of this Act.

(2) An order under subsection (1) may–

(a) contain such savings or transitional provisions as the Secretary of State thinks fit;

(b) make different provision for different purposes.

(3) The power to make an order under subsection (1) shall be exercisable by statutory instrument subject to annulment in pursuance of a resolution of either House of Parliament.

General

22.—(1) This Act may be cited as the Party Wall etc. Act 1996.

(2) This Act shall come into force in accordance with provision made by the Secretary of State by order made by statutory instrument.

(3) An order under subsection (2) may–

(a) contain such savings or transitional provisions as the Secretary of State thinks fit;

(b) make different provision for different purposes.

(4) This Act extends to England and Wales only.

Land Registration Act 2002 (c.9)

60 Boundaries

(1) The boundary of a registered estate as shown for the purposes of the register is a general boundary, unless shown as determined under this section.

(2) A general boundary does not determine the exact line of the boundary.

(3) Rules may make provision enabling or requiring the exact line of the boundary of a registered estate to be determined and may, in particular, make provision about–

(a) the circumstances in which the exact line of a boundary may or must be determined,

(b) how the exact line of a boundary may be determined,

(c) procedure in relation to applications for determination, and

(d) the recording of the fact of determination in the register or the index maintained under section 68.

(4) Rules under this section must provide for applications for determination to be made to the registrar.

Part 9
Adverse Possession

96 Disapplication of periods of limitation

(1) No period of limitation under section 15 of the Limitation Act 1980 (c. 58) (time limits in relation to recovery of land) shall run against any person, other than a chargee, in relation to an estate in land or rentcharge the title to which is registered.

(2) No period of limitation under section 16 of that Act (time limits in relation to redemption of land) shall run against any person in relation to such an estate in land or rentcharge.

(3) Accordingly, section 17 of that Act (extinction of title on expiry of time limit) does not operate to extinguish the title of any person where, by virtue of this section, a period of limitation does not run against him.

97 Registration of adverse possessor

Schedule 6 (which makes provision about the registration of an adverse possessor of an estate in land or rentcharge) has effect.

98 Defences

(1) A person has a defence to an action for possession of land if–

    (a) on the day immediately preceding that on which the action was brought he was entitled to make an application under paragraph 1 of Schedule 6 to be registered as the proprietor of an estate in the land, and

    (b) had he made such an application on that day, the condition in paragraph 5(4) of that Schedule would have been satisfied.

(2) A judgment for possession of land ceases to be enforceable at the end of the period of two years beginning with the date of the judgment if the proceedings in which the judgment is given were commenced against a person who was at that time entitled to make an application under paragraph 1 of Schedule 6.

(3) A person has a defence to an action for possession of land if on the day immediately preceding that on which the action was brought he was entitled to make an application under paragraph 6 of Schedule 6 to be registered as the proprietor of an estate in the land.

(4) A judgment for possession of land ceases to be enforceable at the end of the period of two years beginning with the date of the judgment if, at the end of that period, the person against whom the judgment was given is entitled to make an application under paragraph 6 of Schedule 6 to be registered as the proprietor of an estate in the land.

(5) Where in any proceedings a court determines that–

    (a) a person is entitled to a defence under this section, or

    (b) a judgment for possession has ceased to be enforceable against a person by virtue of subsection (4),

the court must order the registrar to register him as the proprietor of the estate in relation to which he is entitled to make an application under Schedule 6.

(6) The defences under this section are additional to any other defences a person may have.

(7) Rules may make provision to prohibit the recovery of rent due under a rentcharge from a person who has been in adverse possession of the rentcharge.

Schedule 6

Registration of Adverse Possessor

Right to apply for registration

1   (1) A person may apply to the registrar to be registered as the proprietor of a registered estate in land if he has been in adverse possession of the estate for the period of ten years ending on the date of the application.

(2) A person may also apply to the registrar to be registered as the proprietor of a registered estate in land if–

(a) he has in the period of six months ending on the date of the application ceased to be in adverse possession of the estate because of eviction by the registered proprietor, or a person claiming under the registered proprietor,

(b) on the day before his eviction he was entitled to make an application under sub-paragraph (1), and

(c) the eviction was not pursuant to a judgment for possession.

(3) However, a person may not make an application under this paragraph if–

(a) he is a defendant in proceedings which involve asserting a right to possession of the land, or

(b) judgment for possession of the land has been given against him in the last two years.

(4) For the purposes of sub-paragraph (1), the estate need not have been registered throughout the period of adverse possession.

Notification of application

2   (1) The registrar must give notice of an application under paragraph 1 to–

(a) the proprietor of the estate to which the application relates,

(b) the proprietor of any registered charge on the estate,

(c) where the estate is leasehold, the proprietor of any superior registered estate,

(d) any person who is registered in accordance with rules as a person to be notified under this paragraph, and

(e) such other persons as rules may provide.

(2) Notice under this paragraph shall include notice of the effect of paragraph 4.

Treatment of application

3 (1) A person given notice under paragraph 2 may require that the application to which the notice relates be dealt with under paragraph 5.

(2) The right under this paragraph is exercisable by notice to the registrar given before the end of such period as rules may provide.

4 If an application under paragraph 1 is not required to be dealt with under paragraph 5, the applicant is entitled to be entered in the register as the new proprietor of the estate.

5 (1) If an application under paragraph 1 is required to be dealt with under this paragraph, the applicant is only entitled to be registered as the new proprietor of the estate if any of the following conditions is met.

(2) The first condition is that–

(a) it would be unconscionable because of an equity by estoppel for the registered proprietor to seek to dispossess the applicant, and

(b) the circumstances are such that the applicant ought to be registered as the proprietor.

(3) The second condition is that the applicant is for some other reason entitled to be registered as the proprietor of the estate.

(4) The third condition is that–

(a) the land to which the application relates is adjacent to land belonging to the applicant,

(b) the exact line of the boundary between the two has not been determined under rules under section 60,

(c) for at least ten years of the period of adverse possession ending on the date of the application, the applicant (or any predecessor in title) reasonably believed that the land to which the application relates belonged to him, and

(d) the estate to which the application relates was registered more than one year prior to the date of the application.

(5) In relation to an application under paragraph 1(2), this paragraph has effect as if the reference in sub-paragraph (4)(c) to the date of the application were to the day before the date of the applicant's eviction.

Right to make further application for registration

6 (1) Where a person's application under paragraph 1 is rejected, he may make a further application to be registered as the proprietor of the estate if he is in adverse possession of the estate from the date of the application until the last day of the period of two years beginning with the date of its rejection.

(2) However, a person may not make an application under this paragraph if–

(a) he is a defendant in proceedings which involve asserting a right to possession of the land,

(b) judgment for possession of the land has been given against him in the last two years, or

(c) he has been evicted from the land pursuant to a judgment for possession.

7 If a person makes an application under paragraph 6, he is entitled to be entered in the register as the new proprietor of the estate.

Restriction on applications

8 (1) No one may apply under this Schedule to be registered as the proprietor of an estate in land during, or before the end of twelve months after the end of, any period in which the existing registered proprietor is for the purposes of the Limitation (Enemies and War Prisoners) Act 1945 (8 & 9 Geo. 6 c. 16)–

(a) an enemy, or

(b) detained in enemy territory.

(2) No-one may apply under this Schedule to be registered as the proprietor of an estate in land during any period in which the existing registered proprietor is–

(a) unable because of mental disability to make decisions about issues of the kind to which such an application would give rise, or

(b) unable to communicate such decisions because of mental disability or physical impairment.

(3) For the purposes of sub-paragraph (2), "mental disability" means a disability or disorder of the mind or brain, whether permanent or temporary, which results in an impairment or disturbance of mental functioning.

(4) Where it appears to the registrar that sub-paragraph (1) or (2) applies in relation to an estate in land, he may include a note to that effect in the register.

Effect of registration

9   (1) Where a person is registered as the proprietor of an estate in land in pursuance of an application under this Schedule, the title by virtue of adverse possession which he had at the time of the application is extinguished.

(2) Subject to sub-paragraph (3), the registration of a person under this Schedule as the proprietor of an estate in land does not affect the priority of any interest affecting the estate.

(3) Subject to sub-paragraph (4), where a person is registered under this Schedule as the proprietor of an estate, the estate is vested in him free of any registered charge affecting the estate immediately before his registration.

(4) Sub-paragraph (3) does not apply where registration as proprietor is in pursuance of an application determined by reference to whether any of the conditions in paragraph 5 applies.

Apportionment and discharge of charges

10   (1) Where–

(a) a registered estate continues to be subject to a charge notwithstanding the registration of a person under this Schedule as the proprietor, and

(b) the charge affects property other than the estate,

the proprietor of the estate may require the chargee to apportion the amount secured by the charge at that time between the estate and the other property on the basis of their respective values.

(2) The person requiring the apportionment is entitled to a discharge of his estate from the charge on payment of–

(a) the amount apportioned to the estate, and

(b) the costs incurred by the chargee as a result of the apportionment.

(3) On a discharge under this paragraph, the liability of the chargor to the chargee is reduced by the amount apportioned to the estate.

(4) Rules may make provision about apportionment under this paragraph, in particular, provision about–

(a) procedure,

(b) valuation,

(c) calculation of costs payable under sub-paragraph (2)(b), and

(d) payment of the costs of the chargor.

Meaning of "adverse possession"

11   (1) A person is in adverse possession of an estate in land for the purposes of this Schedule if, but for section 96, a period of limitation under section 15 of the Limitation Act 1980 (c. 58) would run in his favour in relation to the estate.

(2) A person is also to be regarded for those purposes as having been in adverse possession of an estate in land–

(a) where he is the successor in title to an estate in the land, during any period of adverse possession by a predecessor in title to that estate, or

(b) during any period of adverse possession by another person which comes between, and is continuous with, periods of adverse possession of his own.

(3) In determining whether for the purposes of this paragraph a period of limitation would run under section 15 of the Limitation Act 1980, there are to be disregarded–

(a) the commencement of any legal proceedings, and

(b) paragraph 6 of Schedule 1 to that Act.

Trusts

12   A person is not to be regarded as being in adverse possession of an estate for the purposes of this Schedule at any time when the estate is subject to a trust, unless the interest of each of the beneficiaries in the estate is an interest in possession.

Crown foreshore

13   (1) Where–

(a) a person is in adverse possession of an estate in land,

(b) the estate belongs to Her Majesty in right of the Crown or the Duchy of Lancaster or to the Duchy of Cornwall, and

(c) the land consists of foreshore,

paragraph 1(1) is to have effect as if the reference to ten years were to sixty years.

(2) For the purposes of sub-paragraph (1), land is to be treated as foreshore if it has been foreshore at any time in the previous ten years.

(3) In this paragraph, "foreshore" means the shore and bed of the sea and of any tidal water, below the line of the medium high tide between the spring and neap tides.

Rentcharges

14   Rules must make provision to apply the preceding provisions of this Schedule to registered rentcharges, subject to such modifications and exceptions as the rules may provide.

Procedure

15   Rules may make provision about the procedure to be followed pursuant to an application under this Schedule.

Appendix 2
Pleadings and other
documents

1. Claim form (Form N1)

	Claim Form	In the	
		Claim No.	

Claimant

SEAL

Defendant(s)

Brief details of claim

Value

Defendant's name and address

£

Amount claimed	
Court fee	
Solicitor's costs	
Total amount	
Issue date	

The court office at

is open between 10 am and 4 pm Monday to Friday. When corresponding with the court, please address forms or letters to the Court Manager and quote the claim number.

N1 Claim form (CPR Part 7) (4.99)   *Printed on behalf of The Court Service*

Claim No.

Does, or will, your claim include any issues under the Human Rights Act 1998? ☐ Yes ☐ No

Particulars of Claim (attached)(to follow)

Statement of Truth
*(I believe)(The Claimant believes) that the facts stated in these particulars of claim are true.
* I am duly authorised by the claimant to sign this statement

Full name _____

Name of claimant's solicitor's firm _____

signed _____ position or office held _____
*(Claimant)(Litigation friend)(Claimant's solicitor) (if signing on behalf of firm or company)
*delete as appropriate

Claimant's or claimant's solicitor's address to
which documents or payments should be sent if
different from overleaf including (if appropriate)
details of DX, fax or e-mail.

Brief details of claim

Note: The facts and full details about your claim and whether or not you are claiming interest, should be set out in the 'particulars of claim' *(see note under 'Particulars of Claim').*

You must set out under **this** heading:

* a concise statement of the nature of your claim
* the remedy you are seeking e.g. payment of money; an order for return of goods or their value; an order to prevent a person doing an act; damages for personal injuries.

Value

If you are claiming a **fixed amount of money** (a 'specified **a**mount') write the amount in the box at the bottom right-hand corner of the claim form against 'amount claimed'.

If you are **not** claiming a fixed amount of money (an 'unspecified amount') under 'Value' write "I expect to recover" followed by whichever of the following applies to your claim:

* "not more than £5,000" or
* "more than £5,000 but not more than £15,000"or
* "more than £15,000"

you are **not able** to put a value on your claim, write "I cannot say how much I expect to recover".

Personal injuries

If your claim is for 'not more than £5,000' and includes a claim for personal injuries, you must also write "My claim includes a claim for personal injuries and the amount I expect to recover as damages for pain, suffering and loss of amenity is" followed by either:

* "not more than £1,000" or
* "more than £1,000"

Housing disrepair

If your claim is for 'not more than £5,000' and includes a claim for housing disrepair relating to residential premises, you must also write "My claim includes a claim against my landlord for housing disrepair relating to residential premises. The cost of the repairs or other work is estimated be" followed by either:

* "not more than £1,000" or
* "more than £1,000"

If within this claim, you are making a claim for other damages, you must also write:

"I expect to recover as damages" followed by either:

* "not more than £1,000" or
* "more than £1,000"

Issuing in the High Court

You may only issue in the High Court if one of the following statements applies to your claim:-

"By law, my claim must be issued in the High Court. The Act which provides this is ....(specify Act)"

or

"I expect to recover more than £15,000"

or

"My claim includes a claim for personal injuries and the value of the claim is £50,000 or more"

or

"My claim needs to be in a specialist High Court list, namely...............................(state which list)".

If one of the statements does apply and you wish to, or must by law, issue your claim in the High Court, write the words "I wish my claim to issue in the High Court because" followed by the relevant statement e.g. "I wish my claim to issue in the High Court because my claim includes a claim for personal injuries and the value of my claim is £50,000 or more."

Defendant's name and address

Enter in this box the full names and address of the defendant receiving the claim form (ie. one claim form for each defendant). If the defendant is to be served outside England and Wales, you may need to obtain the court's permission.

Particulars of claim

You may include your particulars of claim on the claim form in the space provided or in a separate document which you should head 'Particulars of Claim'. It should include the names of the parties, the court, the claim number and your address for service and also contain a statement of truth. You should keep a copy for yourself, provide one for the court and one for each defendant. Separate particulars of claim can either be served

* with the claim form **or**
* within 14 days after the date on which the claim form was served.

If your particulars of claim are served separately from the claim form, they must be served with the forms on which the defendant may reply to your claim.

Your particulars of claim must include

* a concise statement of the facts on which you rely
* a statement (if applicable) to the effect that you are seeking aggravated damages or exemplary damages
* details of any interest which you are claiming
* any other matters required for your type of claim as set out in the relevant practice direction

Address for documents

Insert in this box the address at which you wish to receive documents and/or payments, if different from the address you have already given under the heading 'Claimant'. The address must be in England or Wales. If you are willing to accept service by DX, fax or e-mail, add details.

Statement of truth

This must be signed by you, by your solicitor or your litigation friend, as appropriate.

Where the claimant is a registered company or a corporation the claim must be signed by either the director, treasurer, secretary, chief executive, manager or other officer of the company or (in the case of a corporation) the mayor, chairman, president or town clerk.

Notes for claimant on completing a claim form
Further information may be obtained from the court in a series of free leaflets.

- Please read all of these guidance notes before you begin completing the claim form. The notes follow the order in which information is required on the form.
- Court staff can help you fill in the claim form and give information about procedure once it has been issued. But they cannot give legal advice. If you need legal advice, for example, about the likely success of your claim or the evidence you need to prove it, you should contact a solicitor or a Citizens Advice Bureau.
- If you are filling in the claim form by hand, please use black ink and write in block capitals.
- Copy the completed claim form and the defendant's notes for guidance so that you have one copy for yourself, one copy for the court and one copy for each defendant. Send or take the forms to the court office with the appropriate fee. The court will tell you how much this is.

Notes on completing the claim form

Heading

You must fill in the heading of the form to indicate whether you want the claim to be issued in a county court or in the High Court (The High Court means either a District Registry (attached to a county court) or the Royal Courts of Justice in London). There are restrictions on claims which may be issued in the High Court (see 'Value' overleaf).

Use whichever of the following is appropriate:

'In the ....County Court'
(inserting the name of the court)

or

'In the High Court of Justice......................Division'
(inserting eg. 'Queen's Bench' or 'Chancery' as appropriate)

'.............................District Registry'
(inserting the name of the District Registry)

or

'In the High Court of Justice......................Division,
(inserting eg. 'Queen's Bench' or 'Chancery' as appropriate)
Royal Courts of Justice'

Claimant and defendant details

As the person issuing the claim, you are called the 'claimant'; the person you are suing is called the 'defendant'. Claimants who are under 18 years old (unless otherwise permitted by the court) and patients within the meaning of the Mental Health Act 1983, must have a litigation friend to issue and conduct court proceedings on their behalf. Court staff will tell you more about what you need to do if this applies to you.

You must provide the following information about yourself and the defendant according to the capacity in which you are suing and in which the defendant is being sued. When suing or being sued as:-

an individual:

All known forenames and surname, whether Mr, Mrs, Miss, Ms or Other (e.g. Dr) and residential address (**including** postcode and telephone number) in England and Wales. Where the defendant is a proprietor of a business, a partner in a firm or an individual sued in the name of a club or other unincorporated association, the address for service should be the usual or last known place of residence **or** principal place of business of the company, firm or club or other unincorporated association.

Where the individual is:

under 18 write '(a child by Mr Joe Bloggs his litigation friend)' after the name. If the child is conducting proceedings on their own behalf write '(a child)' after the child's name.

a patient within the meaning of the Mental Health Act 1983 write '(by Mr Joe Bloggs his litigation friend)' after the patient's name.

trading under another name

you must add the words 'trading as' and the trading name e.g. 'Mr John Smith trading as Smith's Groceries'.

suing or being sued in a representative capacity

you must say what that capacity is e.g. 'Mr Joe Bloggs as the representative of Mrs Sharon Bloggs (deceased)'.

suing or being sued in the name of a club or other unincorporated association

add the words 'suing/sued on behalf of' followed by the name of the club or other unincorporated association.

a firm

enter the name of the firm followed by the words 'a firm' e.g. 'Bandbox - a firm' and an address for service which is either a partner's residential address or the principal or last known place of business.

a corporation (other than a company)

enter the full name of the corporation and the address which is either its principal office **or** any other place where the corporation carries on activities and which has a real connection with the claim.

a company registered in England and Wales

enter the name of the company and an address which is either the company's registered office **or** any place of business that has a real, or the most, connection with the claim e.g. the shop where the goods were bought.

an overseas company (defined by s744 of the Companies Act 1985)

enter the name of the company and either the address registered under s691 of the Act **or** the address of the place of business having a real, or the most, connection with the claim.

This form can be downloaded from the court service website www.courtservice.gov.uk.

2. Application notice (Form N244)

Application Notice

In the

Claim no.

Warrant no.
(If applicable)

Claimant
(including ref.)

Defendant(s)
(including ref.)

Date

You should provide this information for listing the application

1. How do you wish to have your application dealt with

   a) at a hearing? ☐ ⎫

   b) at a telephone conference? ☐ ⎬ *complete all questions below*

   c) without a hearing? ☐ *complete Qs 5 and 6 below*

2. Give a time estimate for the hearing/conference
   ____(hours)____(mins)

3. Is this agreed by all parties? ☐ Yes ☐ No

4. Give dates of any trial period or fixed trial date _____

5. Level of judge _____

6. Parties to be served _____

Note You must complete Parts A **and** B, **and** Part C if applicable. Send any relevant fee and the completed application to the court with any draft order, witness statement or other evidence; and sufficient copies for service on each respondent.

Part A

1. Enter your full name, or name of solicitor
I (We)[1]   (on behalf of)(the claimant)(the defendant)

2. State clearly what order you are seeking and if possible attach a draft
intend to apply for an order (a draft of which is attached) that[2]

because[3]

3. Briefly set out why you are seeking the order. Include the material facts on which you rely, identifying any rule or statutory provision

Part B

I (We) wish to rely on: *tick one box*

the attached (witness statement)(affidavit) ☐   my statement of case ☐

4. If you are not already a party to the proceedings, you must provide an address for service of documents
evidence in Part C in support of my application ☐

Signed _____   **Position or office held** _____

(Applicant)('s Solicitor)('s litigation friend)   (if signing on behalf of firm or company)

Address to which documents about this claim should be sent (including reference if appropriate)[4]

	if applicable
	fax no.
	DX no.
	e-mail

Tel. no. _____ Postcode _____

The court office at

is open from 10am to 4pm Monday to Friday. When corresponding with the court please address forms or letters to the Court Manager and quote the claim number.

N244 Application Notice (4.00)   *Printed on behalf of The Court Service*

Part C

Claim No. [   ]

I (We) wish to rely on the following evidence in support of this application:

Statement of Truth

*(I believe) *(The applicant believes) that the facts stated in Part C are true

*delete as appropriate

Signed [   ]

(Applicant)('s Solicitor)('s litigation friend)

Position or office held [   ]

(if signing on behalf of firm or company)

Date [   ]

This form can be downloaded from the court service website www.courtservice.gov.uk

3. Application for injunction (Form N16A)

Application for Injunction (General Form)

In the

Between
_____

☐ Claimant
☐ Applicant
☐ Petitioner
(Tick whichever applies)
☐ Defendant
☐ Respondent

County Court

Claim No.

Claimant's Ref.

and

Defendant's Ref.

Notes on completion

Tick whichever box applies and specify legislation where appropriate

(1) Enter the full name of the person making the application

(2) Enter the full name of the person the injunction is to be directed to

(3) Set out here the proposed restraining orders (if the defendant is a limited company delete the wording in brackets and insert "whether by its servants, agents, officers or otherwise")

(4) Set out here any proposed mandatory orders requiring acts to be done

(5) Set out here any further terms asked for including provision for costs

(6) Enter the names of all persons who have sworn affidavits or signed statement in support of this application

(7) Enter the names and addresses of all persons upon whom it is intended to serve this application

(8) Enter the full name and address for service and delete as required

☐ By application in pending proceedings
☐ Under Statutory provision _____

Seal

This application raises issues under the Human Rights Act 1998   ☐ Yes   ☐ No

The Claimant (Applicant/Petitioner)[1]

applies to the court for an injunction order in the following terms:

That the Defendant (Respondent)[2]

be forbidden (whether by himself or by instructing or encouraging any other person[3]

And that the Defendant(Respondent)[4]

And that[5]

The grounds of this application are set out in the written evidence of[6]   sworn (signed) on

This written evidence is served with this application.
This application is to be served upon[7]

This application is filed by[8]

(the Solicitors for) the Claimant (Applicant/Petitioner)

whose address for service is

Signed   Dated

*   To*
Name and   of
address of   **This application will be heard by the (District) Judge**
the person   **at**
application   **on   the   day of   [20   ]   at   o'clock**
is directed
to   **If you do not attend at the time shown the court may make an injunction order in your absence**

This section to be completed by the court

If you do not fully understand this application you should go to a Solicitor, Legal Advice Centre or a Citizens' Advice Bureau

The court office at

is open between 10am and 4pm Mon - Fri. When corresponding with the court, please address all forms and letters to the Court Manager and quote the claim number.

N16A   General form of application for injunction (10.00)   *The Court Service Publications Unit*

4. Injunction order (Form N16(1))

GENERAL FORM OF INJUNCTION (FORMAL PARTS ONLY)　　N16(1)

Injunction Order

| Between _____ | Claimant
Applicant
Petitioner |
| and _____ | Defendant
Respondent |

In the	County Court
Claim No.	
Claimant	
Defendant	
Claimant's Ref.	
For completion by the court Issued on	

To (1)

of (2)

(Seal)

(1) The name of the person the order is directed to

If you do not obey this order you will be guilty of contempt of court and you may be sent to prison

(2) The address of the person the order is directed to

On　　the　　of　　　　　　[19　][20　]　　　the court considered an application for an injunction

(3) The terms of any restraining order are to be preceeded by the words "is forbidden whether by himself or by instructing or encouraging any other person" or if the defendant is a limited company "by its servants, agents, officers or otherwise"

The Court ordered that[1]

(3)

If you do not understand anything in this order you should go to a Solicitor, Legal Advice Centre or a Citizens' Advice Bureau

---

The court office at

is open between 10 am and 4 pm Monday to Friday. When corresponding with the court. please address forms or letters to the Court Manager and quote the claim number.

N16(1)　　General form of injunction for interlocutory application or originating application (January 2002) Crown Copyright. Reproduced by Sweet & Maxwell Ltd.
(Formal Parts – See complete N16 for wording of operative clauses)

3/10　　　　　　　　　Civil Procedure Forms R.O: March 2002

N16(1)   GENERAL FORM OF INJUNCTION (FORMAL PARTS ONLY)

Injunction Order – Record of Hearing   Claim No._____

On_____the_____day of_____[19][20]_____
Before (H   Honour) (District) Judge _____
The court was sitting at _____

The ☐ Claimant ☐ Applicant ☐ Petitioner (Name)_____
was ☐ represented by Counsel
     ☐ represented by a Solicitor
     ☐ in person
The ☐ Defendant ☐ Respondent   (Name)_____
was ☐ represented by Counsel
     ☐ represented by a Solicitor
     ☐ in person
     ☐ did not appear having been given notice of this hearing
     ☐ not given notice of this hearing

The court read the affidavit(s) of
☐ the Claimant/Applicant/Petitioner   sworn on _____
☐ the Defendant/Respondent   sworn on _____
And of _____ sworn on _____

The court heard spoken evidence on oath from

_____

_____

The Claimant (Applicant/Petitioner) gave an undertaking (through his counsel or
solicitor) promising to pay any damages ordered by the court if it later decides that the
Defendant/Respondent has suffered loss or damage as a result of this order*

Delete this paragraph if the court does not require the undertaking

Signed_   Dated
       (Judges Clerk)

N16(1)   General form of injunction for interlocutory application or originating application under Order 47 rule 8(2)
          (January 2002) Crown Copyright. Reproduced by Sweet & Maxwell Ltd.
          (Formal Parts – See complete N16 for wording of operative clauses)

5. Particulars of claim in a boundary dispute

IN THE POMFRITE COUNTY COURT   Claim No.

BETWEEN:

WINIFRED JOAN BATTLE   Claimant

And

RONALD PETER LEE   Defendant

PARTICULARS OF CLAIM[89]

1. The claimant is and has been at all material times the freehold owner of the land at Vickers Close, Brothertown, North Tyneside shown on the plan annexed hereto edged in red, which is registered with H.M. Land Registry under title number NTY151000 ("the red edged land").

2. By a deed of transfer dated the 19th April 1994 Richard Ian Bradbury conveyed to the claimant the red edged land, which comprised the land referred to in a deed of gift dated 19th July 1991 and secondly the land referred to in a deed of ascent dated 10th March 1993. The claimant will rely on the said deed and on the said ascent for their full terms and effect.

3. The defendant is the freehold owner of the freehold land adjoining the red edged land at its north eastern boundary shown on the plan annexed hereto edged in green, which is registered with HM Land Registry under title number NTY68966 ("the green edged land").

---

89. These may be included on form N1 or attached to that form. Alternatively they may follow within 14 days of the day on which the claim form is served (CPR 7.4(1)(b)).

4. On a date early in 1992 the defendant wrongfully trespassed upon the red edged land and constructed a greenhouse thereon without the permission of the claimant's predecessor in title, the said Richard Ian Bradley.

5. The said greenhouse remains in situ despite the claimant's requests that he should remove the same on [SET OUT ANY LETTERS REQUESTING THE DEFENDANT TO REMOVE THE GARAGE].

5. By reason of the defendant's said trespass the claimant has suffered distress, inconvenience, loss and damage.

PARTICULARS OF SPECIAL DAMAGE

Estimated cost of removing the garage and restoring the claimant's land as a garden and all works incidental thereto:

£...

6. The claimant is entitled to and claims interest pursuant to section 69 of the County Courts Act 1984 upon any damages which may be recovered at such rate and for such period as the Court thinks fit.

AND the claimant claims:–

(1) A declaration that she is the freehold owner of the red edged land.

(2) An injunction to restrain the defendant, whether by himself or through his servants or agents, from entering upon the red edged land or otherwise interfering with the claimant's occupation thereof.

(3) An order that the defendant do forthwith remove the greenhouse currently lying on the claimant's land and reinstate the land to its former condition.

(4) Damages limited to £5,000.[90]

(5) Interest thereon.

(6) Costs.

W.E. Gladstone

Dated this   day of   200 .

---

90. It is a requirement of CPR 16.3 that the claimant shall endorse the amount he expects to recover on the claim form and it is customary to put a similar endorsement on the particulars of claim and where the damages cannot be precisely quantified (because they are an item of general damage to be determined by the trial judge) it is cutomary to state that the claim is limited, e.g. to £5,000.

Statement of Truth

The Claimant believes that the contents of these particulars of claim are true.

Full name _____

Name of claimant's solicitor's firm _____

Signed _____ Position held _____

By: Fartle and Worsthome, Garrygate Chambers, Pomfrite, West Hartlepool HP12 1SE.

Solicitors for the claimant.

Claimant's solitor's address to which documents should be sent

6. Advice to accompany particulars of claim at 5 in a boundary dispute

WINNIFRED JOAN BATTLE

And

RONALD PETER LEE

ADVICE

1. My instructing solicitor will find enclosed a draft Particulars of Claim in this matter. It should be noted that prior to issue two gaps in the pleading will need to be filled.

Facts/Conveyancing history

2. Mrs Battle is the freehold owner of 1 Vicars Close, Brothertown, North Tyneside together with the small plot close to her home which was formerly owned by the Bradley family. That plot was transferred to her by a deed of transfer dated 19th April 1994 and has been registered with title absolute at H.M. Land Registry under title number NYK151000. The root of title to this small plot can be traced by referring to the epitome of title helpfully obtained by my instructing solicitor. However, it is necessary to look no further than the deed of gift dated the 19th July 1991 and the ascent dated the 10th March 1993. These documents make it plain that Mrs Battle's north eastern boundary ends at the old site of 8 Vicars Close. I understand that Mr Lee is now the owner of this site and has built a garage on it. According to the epitome he is also the owner of a plot of land lying to the south west end of Vicars Close and of 1 Vicars Close itself, the precise boundary to which is not identified on the documents before me.

Ownership of the disputed land

3. Title absolute was granted on 22nd April 1994 and there does not appear, on the documents before me, to be any dispute as to Mrs Battle's good title. Bearing in mind the root of title can be traced back through the Bradley family over a number of generations this is not surprising. The effect of first registration is to vest Mrs Battle with the fee simple in the land (section 5 of the Land Registration Act 1925). However this statement has to be qualified in the sense that normal registration shows only the general boundaries (Rule 278 of the Land Registration Rules 1925). Therefore the boundaries as shown on the Land Registry plan may not be completely accurate.

4. There are a number of features of this case which assist in this regard. Firstly the history of the title seems to be fairly well documented. Secondly it seems that the boundary is straight and follows the line of the former row of cottages. Thirdly the physical features of the site suggest the approximate edge of Mrs Battle's title. It is therefore difficult to see how Mr Lee could effectively dispute the boundary. His own boundary is well established over a long period and the area he is presently occupying with his greenhouse cannot be the site of number 8 Vicars Close since that site is, as I understand it, entirely taken up with the garage.

5. I have not seen any correspondence with Mr Lee so that I know not what case he is putting forward, but I assume that his construction of the greenhouse arises out of some attempt to claim adverse possession. The only other basis upon which I can see him claiming possession of the land is on the basis of some acquiescence or estoppel on the part of one of Mrs Battle's predecessors in title. It is pointless commenting on such arguments until it is known what case he is putting forward.

The evidence

6. Turning to the state of the evidence, I note that a number of the statutory declarations are not signed. It will be necessary to have them signed before they can be referred to in the proceedings. It should be noted that before they can be used in court the necessary Civil Evidence Act notices must accompany them as with any other hearsay evidence. Alternatively the witnesses must be called to give evidence.

7. Secondly I found it very difficult to understand the layout of this complex site and the case would very much benefit from having a measured site plan indicating the exact location of the surviving outbuildings and the relationship of the various boundaries to the registered titles in existence. Since this is an expensive undertaking and I understand that Mrs Battle

has limited funds with which to fight this case, a cheaper alternative to this is to obtain a clear set of photographs, which can be related to the boundaries in existence. These should show clearly the angle that they are taken from and related to the plan. My instructing solicitor should also try to obtain an enlarged copy of the more detailed of the two Land Registry plans, and mark on it all the registered and unregistered titles in existence at the site.

8. Finally it is always helpful in a case of this kind to have a site visit so that I may get a fuller idea of the layout of the site. However, I fully understand that resources may not permit such a visit at this stage. In the meantime I should be pleased to assist further with any other matters that arises on the telephone.

W.E. Gladstone

Parliament Chambers
22 Downing Parade
Leigh
Lancs.
L7 5BP.

7. Skeleton argument in adverse possession claim

IN THE BARNLEY COUNTY COURT

Claim No. BY0100616

BETWEEN:–

MARK DARREN ANTHONY (1)
DORRIS CLEOPATRA PRATT (2)

And

<u>Claimants</u>

REGINALD IOLANTHE PERRIN

<u>Defendant</u>

CLAIMANTS' SKELETON ARGUMENT

Introduction

1. Cs are the freehold owners of the Goat Public House, Chapel Road, Tinley. D lives at the next but one house (number 77, Chapel Road, Tinley) (see 43). As will be seen from the chronology at 1a, D acquired title to his land in or about August 1985 and within the first year of his ownership claims that he agreed that he would have use of a greenhouse in the north west corner of Cs' land (known as "the disputed land") with Mr Roehampton, then the licensee of the Goat Inn. This is disputed; indeed, the Cs say that the greenhouse was actually sold to a Mr Crookes by Mr Roehampton.

2.   Cs became tenants of the Goat Inn in 1988 and acquired freehold title by a transfer in October 1991. In May 1998 they sought permission to erect a single dwelling but this was refused. D did object to that application (but N.B. the basis of his objection (at 32)).

3.   The *chronology* therefore is as follows:

   8/85   D purchases his property

   1988   Cs become licensee of the Goat

   1991   Cs purchase the freehold

   7/5/92   Cs' offer of licence to permit greenhouse to remain on Cs' land

   6/7/92   Cs' solicitors request removal of greenhouse

   5/5/98   Cs' planning application

   3/00   D began to use disputed land on a regular basis

   6/4/00   Cs give formal notice of termination of licence (thereafter there is increasing use of the disputed land by D)

   5/00   Cs issue claim form (which stops time running in the D's favour)

4.   It is common ground that the D has made some use of the disputed land and greenhouse but the extent of that occupation and use is disputed. It is disputed that the ingredients needed for a successful adverse possession claim are present.

Issues

5.   The following issues appear to arise:

   1) Was there some agreement to permit the D to use the greenhouse by Mr Roehampton? (The evidence does not appear to establish who erected the greenhouse on the disputed land, it does not appear to have been D or Cs' predecessor).

   2) Did Mr Crookes "buy" the greenhouse off the former licensee of the Gate Mr Roehampton for £1 when he came to leave in 1985/6?

   3) Was there a conversation in 1991, after Cs' bought the Gate Inn, in which D sought permission to use the greenhouse on the disputed land, but was refused?

   4) What acts of possession has D established:

a) Before April 2000, when C served him with notice to terminate the licence, and

b) After April 2000?

5) Were those acts of possession that he is able to prove the subject of a licence, express or implied?

Principles

6. Adverse possession requires exclusive possession coupled with a demonstrable intention to exclude everyone.

7. The first element is therefore the necessary degree of exclusive physical control, which must have been for a period of at least 12 years without interruption so as to defeat the paper title owner's (PTO's) cause of action to recover his land (s.15 LA 1980).

8. The high test that the squatter must surmount is to demonstrate:

    "Complete and exclusive physical control" (Gray '*Elements of Land Law*' 2nd. ed. p.264).

9. The intensity of user required will vary according to the nature of the land involved. But, it must be shown that:

    "The alleged possessor has been dealing with the land in question as an occupying owner might have expected to deal with it and no one else has done so" (*Powell* v *Mc Farlane* at 471).

10. Time may only begin to run in favour of the squatter where there has been discontinuance of possession by the paper title owner and "the rebuttal of a fairly heavy presumption that possession is retained by the paper title owner" (Gray at 259 (see also *Williams Bros Direct Stores* v *Raftery* [1957] 3 All ER 593 and *Wallis's Clayton Bay Holiday Camp Ltd* v *Shell Mex* [1974] 3 All ER 575).

11. The "slightest acts of ownership" on the part of PTO will rebut any suggestion that he has discontinued possession of his land (*Buckingham County Council* v *Moran* [1990] 1 Ch. 623).

12. The second element is the necessary *animus possidendi*, which is:

    1) Discontinuance of possession by the paper title owner; and

    2) "the rebuttal of a fairly heavy presumption that possession is retained by the paper title owner" (Gray at 259 (see also *Williams Bros Direct*

Stores v *Raftery* [1957] 3 All ER 593 and *Wallis's Clayton Bay Holiday Camp Ltd* v *Shell Mex* [1974] 3 All ER 575).

13. The "slightest acts of ownership" on the part of PTO will rebut any suggestion that he has discontinued possession of his land (*Buckingham County Council* v *Moran* [1990] 1 Ch. 623).

14. The second element is the necessary animus possidendi, which is: "The intention in one's own name and on one's own behalf to exclude the world at large" (per Slade J in *Powell* v *Mc Farlane* (1977) 38 P & CR 452).

Submissions

Have Cs or their predecessors discontinued possession of the disputed land?

15. This question must be judged by the nature of the land involved. It is land that is of little amenity value to the Public House and the evidence therefore points to the PTO having limited use for it. However, there is no evidence that that use has been discontinued. The evidence points to this being a convenient area into which D could expand his gardening activities given his own relatively small garden. D himself asserts that C grew cannabis plants on the land, which is fundamentally inconsistent with there having been a cessation of possession by C.

Has D been in exclusive physical control of the disputed land and if so when did such possession begin?

16. There is nothing "exclusive" about the D's occupation and use of the disputed land here, nor did he contend through his solicitors in April 2000, when the licence was terminated, that his possession was "exclusive" (see 36). D's case on adverse possession is inconsistent with:

1) The statement at paragraph 5 of his statement (at 18) to the effect that they agreed that they would have joint use of the greenhouse.

2) The independent evidence of Mr Roehampton, which points to the use of the greenhouse having been shared amongst a number of customers of the Goat (see 14 at Para. 3).

3) The evidence of D himself, which points to C1 having dumped rubbish on it in 1989.

17. The acts relied on would rarely establish the necessary degree of physical control given the character of the land concerned (that can be seen by looking at the photographs (see especially 37)). There has been no attempt to enclose the land in other than the crudest way possible. At most it is shared use, which is consistent with the licence type arrangement referred

to and cannot amount to adverse possession. Even of the court accepts that the D has used the greenhouse for at least twelve years there appears to have been nothing exclusive about it and there has been no use of the surrounding land.

18. His use of the disputed land was de minimis between 1991 and 2000, when the Cs' solicitors withdrew any licence that he had.

19. D's use of the land has not been adverse but was on his own evidence pursuant to a licence, which was orally terminated in 1991. The outcome of such discussion was that D appears to have accepted that he could not "rent" the land, which he sought to do. Such a discussion would only have taken place if the D considered the Cs' to be the owner and does not in any way support D's case that he believed he had the right to exclusive control of the land.

20. The Cs, by their letters in 1992, clearly set out that their understanding of the occupation of the disputed land was pursuant to a licence. The absence of any response was indicative of consent to that proposition.

Had D's possession of the land been with the necessary animus possidendi?

21. The acts of possession described do not lead the court to conclude that the intention to possess may be inferred. On the contrary many of them are ambiguous and are equally consistent with there having been a licence.

22. D did not object to the planning application in 1998 on the basis that he was in possession of that land, which one have expected him to do.

When did time begin to run?

23. Even if the court accepts that at some stage the D has been in exclusive physical control of the disputed land, it could not have begun whilst Mr Roehampton was the licensee (until 1985/6). Nor could it have begun before 1989, when C1 dumped rubbish on it. In Cs' submission shared use continued for much longer and has only ceased in about 2000.

W.E. Gladstone

Dated

Parliament Chambers
22 Downing Parade
Leigh
Lancs.
L7 5BP

8. Part structure notice under section 3 of the Party Wall Act 1996

Party Structure Notice

Party Wall etc Act 1996

To   Mr Phil Pile
Of   2 Dimbleby Drive
    Stoke on Trent

Owner

I   I.M.A. Nuisance
   4 Dimbleby Drive
   toke on Trent

Building Owner

As the owner of 4 Dimbleby Drive, Stoke on Trent (the property) which adjoins your property at 2 Dimbleby Drive, Stoke on Trent

I hereby give you notice that in accordance with my rights under section 2(2) of the above Act I wish to carry out work to the party structure separating the above premises. It is intended to carry out this work within two months from service of this notice.

The proposed works are the complete reconstruction of the existing party wall and removal of the asbestos dust from the roof space of the adjoining structure to ensure future stability, partial rebuilding of the said wall, increasing the height of the adjoining structure so as to allow greater headroom and to accommodate a foul water outlet from the 2nd floor WC.

I intend to commence the above works on 20th April 2003 and to complete them on the 20th April 2060 or earlier by agreement.

Under section 5 of the Act, if you do not consent to the proposed works within 14 days you will have been deemed to dissented and a dispute will have been deemed to have arisen.

Section 10 of the Act requires both parties to concur in the appointment of a surveyor and in those circumstances I would propose that we appoint Mr Tommy Nutt of Bollard and Nutt's Consulting Engineers and Steel Erectors

Signed

20 February 2003

9. Particulars of claim for an access order under the Access to Neighbouring Land Act 1992[91]

IN THE POMFRITE COUNTY COURT   Claim No.

BETWEEN:

WINSTON SPENCER JENKINS

Claimant

And

PETER NADIR

Defendant

PARTICULARS OF CLAIM

---

1.   The claimant is the freehold owner of the dwelling house shown on the plan annexed hereto edged in red ("the dominant land"). The defendant is the owner of the adjoining land edged green on the plan annexed hereto ("the servient land"). Part 8 of the CPR applies to this claim.

2.   The boundary wall that separates the dominant land from the servient land is in a serious state of disrepair. Urgent work is required to that wall to arrest the decline in its condition and to bring the said wall into a satisfactory condition. The work required is particularised in the report

---

91. The Procedure is now governed by CPR PD 56 para 11; the particulars of claim should be under Part 8 of the CPR and should therefore be supported by an appropriate statement.

of Professor van Deelam. The said work cannot be carried out without gaining access to the servient land.

3. The defendant has persistently refused access for the purposes of carrying out the essential work summarised in Professor van Deelam's report and more particularly described on the plans annexed thereto, the latest such request having been made in a letter of 23rd December 2002.

4. Cowbouys Limited, builders and shot putters, of Back Passage, Off Camden High Street, London N1, will carry out the work. If access is granted it could begin on 1st March 2003 and will take approximately 10 weeks to complete.

5. The claimant has a policy of insurance, including all third party risks, with Defo and Co of 1 Lloyds Passage, Stepney, London E1, for the proposed duration of the work.

AND the claimant claims:

1) an access order under section 1 of the Access to Neighbouring Land Act 1992 on the terms herein set out or on such further or other terms as the court may provide.

2) an order for the costs of this application.

W.E. Gladstone

Statement of Truth

The Claimant believes that the contents of these particulars of claim are true.

Full name _____

Name of claimant's solicitor's firm _____

Signed _____ Position held _____

By: Fartle and Worsthome, Garrygate Chambers, Pomfrite, West Hartlepool HP12 1SE.

Solicitors for the claimant.

Claimant's solitor's address to which documents should be sent

Index

more relevant publishing from emis professional publishing

emis professional publishing publishes a range of property and litigation titles for users of *Boundary Disputes*. See over for relevant property titles: here are two of the litigation titles that may be most relevant.

civil appeals

this definitive looseleaf work, edited by the President of the EAT, Sir Michael Burton, contains a chapter on appeals from the county court and Lands Tribunals alongside authoritative sections on appeals from almost every civil tribunal.

£275 – 2 looseleaf volumes and single user electronic version
Available on 28 days approval

civil practice law reports

the only full text reports to focus on matters of procedure, this service provides a citable reference on points of procedure for cases often unreported or reported in specialist reports for other reasons.

Ask for a free sample

legal expenses insurance

All civil litigators and insurers must fully understand the contractual and professional position of lawyers acting for the insured and at the same time taking payment from an insurer. At once practical and accessible and will prove invaluable in an LEI matter.

£28.00   1998   ISBN 1 85811 188 9

For a full range of litigation titles see www.emispp.com

property publishing from emis professional publishing

emis property service

emis's new property service is a unique combination of updating and practical articles presented in a new and exciting combination of media. Together it will keep you up to date with a minimum of effort, and provide an archive of practical "how-to" articles that will help solve your client's problems.

The EMIS Property Service
Incorporating Marplus

Editors:

> John Martin LLB (London), LLM (Michigan), Solicitor, Director of Property Law Research, Pinsent Curtis

> Professor Peter Reekie, solicitor and lecturer

> Brian Kilcoyne BA (Oxon) Law, Solicitor, Lewis Silkin

> Desmond Kilcoyne LLB (Southampton), LLM (London – Commercial Law), Barrister, Arden Chambers

> Guy Williams, Barrister, 2 Mitre Court Buildings

> Qdos Consulting

Property practitioners need incisive, interpretative information that gets to the heart of law and practice.

This new service combines the virtues of several existing services into a new wider service in:

- 12 paper issues per year
- 12 email issues per year
- A fully searchable archive in Seneca EP
- Columns on all aspects of property
- Regular updates on case and legislative developments.

In 2003, subscribers will receive both "how-to" articles and updating materials across the whole range of contentious and non-contentious aspects of property.

Contents include:

- Real property
- Commercial property
- Residential property
- Agriculture
- Planning
- Domestic landlord and tenant
- VAT on Property

Articles will be presented as checklists, notes for guidance on difficult issues, diagrams, points to watch and other formats appropriate to the topic.

Updates will be sent to a designated email address in the first week of every month – which can include any number of email addresses within the subscribing firm.

The Seneca EP electronic service provides a single user licence free within the service to allow the whole archive to be searched at the same time. Your own articles and notes can be added to the records. A network version can be purchased which will allow the firm to share information within the property department.

Pages: 16, A4 Newsletter (12 per annum)
12 e-mail bulletins per annum and single user licence for electronic service
Price: £195 per annum

Boundary Disputes purchasers ask for a two month FREE trial.
Simply ring Rob Owen on 01707 334823 and let us know your postal and email address.

Rights of Way

Simon Blackford, Barrister

Rights of access to land have never been more topical. The Government's Rights to Roam proposals mean that landowners and ramblers alike must look afresh at the issue. Solicitors must offer accurate advice at a time of change. Local government, caught in the middle, must play a difficult hand – advising neutrally in an area likely to stoke passions. Simon Blackford's guide is succinctly written, providing a guide that will be invaluable to all these constituencies.

£24.00   1999   ISBN: 1 85811 166 8

Commercial Leases: 50 Traps for the Unwary

John Martin, LLB (London), LLM (Michigan), Solicitor, Director of Property Law Research, Pinsent Curtis

This unique text brings together, fully referenced and indexed, John Martin's popular short pieces for advisers of landlords and tenants in commercial leases. Written in a clear and authoritative style, the book is laid out in a tried and tested format designed to maximise the usefulness to the practitioner when faced with a particular "Trap". Faced with issues such as a Split Reversion, a "Hybrid" Tenancy or an Either Way Review, potential traps are highlighted, clarified and can be avoided in straightforward fashion. Individuals, solicitors, surveyors, local authority officers and all others involved in the construction or management of property will find the work invaluable.

£38.00   1999   ISBN 185811 218 4

Contaminated Land: Property Transactions and the New Regime

Richard Harwood Barrister, Chambers of Lionel Read QC, 1 Serjeants' Inn

Martin Edwards Barrister, Chambers of Lionel Read QC, 1 Serjeants' Inn

William Upton Barrister, Chambers of Lionel Read QC, 1 Serjeants' Inn

It is essential that property and commercial practitioners fully understand the law and practicalities of dealing with contaminated land. This substantial book puts the new Guidance in its Regulatory context, and interprets it for practitioners.

Key contents: – The new contaminated land regime: How does it work? Who is liable? What does it mean for developers, landowners, local authorities and professionals? – Water, waste and statutory nuisance – Private law rights: nuisance, negligence, Rylands v Fletcher – Planning and contaminated land – Protecting property and corporate transactions.

£42   2000   ISBN 1 85811 206 0

Tenant Default under Commercial leases, Third Edition

Andrew E Parsons Solicitor, Partner, Radcliffes

Tenant default is an area of major concern to landlords and their professional advisers. The cross over of landlord and tenant law and the process of debt collection brings to the fore a series of practical and legal problems for the professional.

Once the tell-tale signs are there – non-payment of rent of a service charge, failure to repair, breach of user covenants or insolvency – prompt action is needed. This book was written to bring together in an easy to use and practical format the materials necessary to effect that action. Succinct and well laid-out chapters provide self-contained explanations of the options available and advice on how to proceed.

Well-drafted Precedents are provided. Changes since the second edition: the Civil Procedure Rules and their accompanying Practice Direction have affected tenant default actions. This edition has been brought thoroughly into line with the Rule and terminological changes that the Reforms have effected, as well as taking into account new law. Individuals, solicitors, surveyors, local authority officers and all others involved in the construction or management of property will find the work invaluable.

£44   2000   ISBN 1 85811 240 0

EMIS Professional Publishing, 31-33 Stonehills House, Welwyn Garden City, AL8 6PU
Tel: 01707 334823   Fax: 01707 335022   DX 144000 Welwyn Garden City
order any title online at *www.emispp.com*

Seneca CM – revolutionary software from emis it

Seneca CM is a complete Contact, file and activity Management system for legal practice. An elegant, one-stop solution that is flexible enough to handle even the most unusual work types, Seneca CM from emis intellectual technology has been intuitively designed to work just the way you do.

Seneca CM is designed to handle any type of file in organisations of any type and size, whether private practice, in-house or local government, including unusual file types. We look at your documents and workflows, and offer a bespoke system to suit your needs.

The system provides a wide range of legal functionality within one single package, including Microsoft Word and digital dictation. Seneca CM allows you to integrate new technology into your contact management, such as multi-media files and biometric technology. Integration with Seneca Electronic Publishing (EP) provides the latest up to date legal information at your fingertips. Seneca EP is included free during the first year of installation of Seneca CM.

For more see *www.emisit.com* or contact us on 08701 225 525